HANDBALL
ILLUSTRATED

D1544126

Charlie O'Connell

THE RONALD PRESS COMPANY • NEW YORK

Library of Congress Catalog Card Number: 64–17554

PRINTED IN THE UNITED STATES OF AMERICA

Foreword

The ancient game of handball has been streamlined and modernized. Glass-walled, air-conditioned, well-illuminated courts are found in increasing numbers around the country. Three-walled courts have been constructed and used successfully. Players use balls that are manufactured to approved specifications. Experimentation has gone forward to develop handball gloves, shoes, and other playing equipment of high-quality material and design. Agreements have been reached between national organizations (Amateur Athletic Union, Young Men's Christian Association, U. S. Handball Association, and National Jewish Welfare Board) making possible one set of Unified Handball Playing Rules. Important matches are reported play by play to large audiences via radio and television. Score sheets and forms have been standardized. When possible, national tournaments are cooperatively scheduled to avoid conflicts in dates and to distribute events to various sections of the country. A key figure in these developments has been Charles J. "Charlie" O'Connell.

Charlie O'Connell was a successful sales executive in a large insurance company, but he has also had time to help thousands of persons develop skill and interest in one-wall, three-wall, and four-wall handball. Since retiring he has worked untiringly with others for the benefit of handball and amateur sport. He has served as chairman of the Amateur Athletic Union's Committee on Handball since 1956.

Charlie is well known to thousands of players and respected by all because of his consideration for others and constant study to improve the game. He edited the A.A.U. Handball Guide for many years, and has written countless articles about the game for papers and periodicals.

The author of this book started playing one-wall handball in the Old Trinity Club at Montague and Clinton Streets in Brooklyn. In the summertime he played against the bulkheads on the hard sand when the tide went out at Brighton Beach in the Coney Island section. He also played in the Park Department and from 1927 to 1935 at the Crescent Club. He has been a member of the New York Athletic Club since 1935 and plays there regularly three times a week.

Dr. Harold T. Friermood
Senior Director for Health and
   Physical Education
National Board of YMCA's

Preface

The purpose of this book is to furnish a guide to beginners. It contains instruction, methods, and suggestions for both one-wall and four-wall handball. An important feature is the verbatim quotations from outstanding national handball champions, explaining their personal approach to the various techniques and giving advice illustrated with action photographs. The players quoted and illustrated include: Vic Hershkowitz, Jimmy Jacobs, John Sloan, Phil Collins, and the Obert brothers—Carl, Oscar, and Ruby. The book should also be of help to all experienced players who desire to improve their game.

Handball is an increasingly popular pastime, played by many thousands of persons of all age groups in every state of the Union. It is a vigorous game for anyone aspiring to tournament competition, but it can be played in moderation by anyone interested only in a pleasant, body-building form of exercise. Handball can be paced to suit the ability, skills, and purposes of the players involved in the particular game.

A game of handball provides considerable physical and mental exercise. It requires the use of both hands and, in this respect, has an advantage over many other games—particularly if you are ambidextrous! Both arms and shoulders are developed and strengthened. The leg, arm, back, and abdominal muscles are brought into play. The game requires quick starts, sudden stops, bending backward, forward, and sideways, as well as stretching and reaching overhead. Mentally, it requires anticipation in playing a ball and concentration in trying to outmaneuver an opponent or force him out of position.

Handball is a convenient game for businessmen, because in almost every city you will find one or more handball courts at the YMCA, YMHA, or at private clubs. A game of handball for forty-five minutes or less offers physical and mental relaxation that is good for body-building and general health. Many businessmen find it convenient to play once or twice during the week at lunch time. For time, handball games are a pleasant and beneficial recreation to look forward to and enjoy. As a method of obtaining a workout in a short time, handball is unsurpassed.

Handball is not confined to men alone; the distaff side has taken to it increasingly as an ideal form of exercise for health and weight control. The extent of this feminine interest in handball is indicated by the report of the New York City Recreation Department, showing that each year approximately 600 women enter the city handball tournaments.

Handball is also played by many professional athletes who are engaged in other sports, such as baseball, football, and basketball, as a means of keeping in good physical condition during their inactive periods.

CHARLIE O'CONNELL

New York, N. Y.
March, 1964

ACKNOWLEDGMENTS

I would like to express my thanks to the great handball champions who have made invaluable contributions to this book. In addition, I wish to acknowledge the material assistance of many well-informed friends in all phases of handball administration and play:

Rev. Daniel F. O'Connell (not related to me), Prefect of Studies at Cathedral College, Brooklyn, N. Y., for his editorial assistance.

Michael M. Rand, Consultant, Health and Physical Education Services, National Jewish Welfare Board, New York City.

Albert Stein, Chairman, National Jewish Welfare Board Handball Committee, and Physical Director of the Ninety-Second Street YMHA, New York City.

Albert Borthwick, for over thirty years Physical Director of the famous Trinity Club of Brooklyn, the "cradle of champions."

Marcus Blechman, Chairman, Metropolitan AAU Handball Committee.

I have frequently drawn from the AAU Official Handball Rules Book for rules, interpretations, and procedures. I am indebted to the United States Handball Association for permission to use the excellent action pictures sent me.

CHARLIE O'CONNELL

Contents

HANDBALL ILLUSTRATED

Introduction

A BRIEF HISTORY OF HANDBALL

Much has been written about the history of handball. It has been traced to the days of the Roman Empire. It was played in the British Isles back in the sixteenth century under the name of "Fives." It is safe to assume that handball really got its start when the first rubber ball was made. The instinctive thing to do with a rubber ball is to bounce it, catch it, and throw it against a wall. Bob Ripley of "Believe It Or Not" fame (and who, by the way, was an excellent player) said: "Handball is the oldest game played with a ball."

It is an accepted fact that handball, as it is played today, is of Celtic origin. In the middle of the nineteenth century records show that county and town championships were held all through the Emerald Isle. It was a very popular game, and as these young Irishmen migrated to the United States, they brought the great game of handball with them.

In the early days the "hard" ball was used. This ball had a cork center about the size of a marble and around this were wound strips of crude rubber, similar to thin rubber bands. A thread or yarn was then applied and wound tightly until the ball had a circumference of approximately that of the present standard "soft" ball. It was then covered with a thin but durable horsehide skin and sewn in practically the same method as a baseball. It then resembled a baseball, but was much smaller in size. When these balls were properly made, they were exceptionally fast, far exceeding the speed of the present standard ball.

The first four-wall championship handball court in the United States was constructed in Brooklyn, N.Y., in 1886 or 1887. It was known as "Casey's Court," and on it were played some of the greatest handball matches in the United States. The court had a slab slate front wall 30 feet high and 25 feet wide, with side walls of cement 65 feet long and a rear

3

wall 12 feet high. It was acknowledged to be one of the finest courts ever constructed in the United States.

In the hard ball game kicking the ball was permitted and those old-time players developed remarkable skill in returning practically all the low balls with their feet.

The first international handball match ever held was between John Lawlor, the champion of Ireland, and Phil Casey, champion of the United States. The match consisted of twenty-one games; ten to be played at Cork, Ireland, and eleven in the United States. The first series took place at Cork on August 4th, 1887. The unusual size of the court (80 by 40) was a handicap to Casey, who was beaten six games to four. The second series was played on November 29th, 1887, on Casey's Court in Brooklyn. The gallery could not begin to accommodate the numbers who desired to

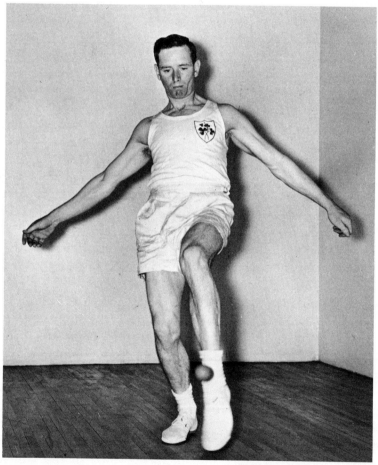

Photo by the New York Daily Mirror

John Ryan of Wexford, Ireland, eleven times holder of the All Ireland Handball Title. John is shown returning the ball with his foot. In Ireland kicking the ball is permissible and it is amazing to see the skill, speed, and control of the ball of these Irish players. Ryan excelled in kicking the ball.

see this match. Casey won seven straight games and the match. He was a wonderful player and was hailed as the champion of the world. He retired undefeated around 1900.

Many famous men succeeded Casey, such as James Dunne, his son Judge James Dunne, Bernard McQuade, Michael Egan, James Kelly, Tom Jones, and many others.

Some few years prior to 1900, a soft ball put in an appearance. It was in the form of a tennis ball with the top covering removed, and was used principally in the smaller four-wall courts throughout New York City. Soon, young men began playing out-of-doors using a brick wall of some building as a back wall. The soft ball rapidly spread to many cities in the United States, but was confined mostly to four-wall. As the players became more familiar with this large tennis-type ball, they soon found it unsatisfactory and wanted a faster ball. So a gas ball, somewhat smaller than a tennis ball, was introduced. The game immediately received an added impetus.

But, as many new soft ball players developed, the large gas ball came into disfavor and a smaller but heavier ball, much faster than the old one, soon made its appearance with satisfactory results.

With the remarkable spread of the game the Middle West came into prominence as the center of soft ball four-wall activities. The Detroit Athletic Club early interested itself in the soft ball game, constructing wonderful four-wall courts, which were duplicated by many YMCA's and athletic clubs. The Detroit Athletic Club can be credited with creating national interest in four-wall play. It invited, at considerable expense, prominent players from various sections of the country to compete for championship honors.

In 1915 the first invitation tournament was held and it was won by Fritz Seivered of Cleveland, who repeated in 1916. Ed Groden, peer of eastern players, won the tournament in 1917. In 1918 another representative of the East, Bill Sakmann, was crowned champion.

While the Detroit Athletic Club was holding these invitational tournaments, four-wall handball was making a strong bid for recognition on the Pacific coast. Los Angeles and San Francisco were represented in local tournaments by excellent players.

In 1919 the Amateur Athletic Union held its first AAU championship in Detroit. Bill Ranft of the Los Angeles Athletic Club played an excellent brand of handball and won the championship. In 1926 the YMCA held its first national championship. The AAU and the YMCA have held national tournaments annually ever since.

In 1951 the United States Handball Association was officially founded with Robert W. Kendler as president. Bob Kendler has made many contributions to the development of handball, principally in his pioneering the use of glass in the construction and remodeling of four-wall courts. His generous support was a major factor in the erection of the beautiful all-glass court at the Aurora, Ill., YMCA. The USHA's *Ace*, devoted entirely to handball news, is a top-flight sports magazine, under the editorship of Mort Leve.

Single-wall handball was first played outdoors at the beach resorts in the Metropolitan New York City area about 1910. Seeing the interest of so many bathers in handball, Mr. Charles J. Kean, manager of the Parkway Baths, Brighton Beach, N.Y., at the suggestion of the author, constructed the first one-wall outdoor handball court. Thus was one-wall handball introduced at the seashore. Within a few years it grew to such an extent that courts were built in the parks and playgrounds throughout the city, where it is the most popular form of exercise and recreation and is played by thousands of young and middle-aged men as well as many young women.

HANDBALL COURTS

There are three officially recognized games of handball, namely: one-wall, three-wall, and four-wall. The AAU, the YMCA, the USHA, and the JWB hold national championships in four-wall. The AAU and the USHA as well each hold national one-wall championships. The USHA holds a national three-wall championship.

One-wall handball is principally confined to the Metropolitan New York City area. It is practically unknown in the Middle West and on the Pacific Coast.

Three-wall courts with front and two side walls, no back wall, are few in number throughout the country. The most popular of these three-wall courts are found in Palmer Park, Detroit, where the USHA holds the championship each year.

Three-wall jai-alai type courts (with front wall, back wall, and one side wall—one side open) are a recent innovation in the parks and playgrounds of New York City. They are the first of their kind in the United States and bring into play all the skills, of back wall and side wall shots, common to four-wall play combined with the accuracy of one-wall handball. The open side permits many spectators to enjoy and watch the skillful shots made by the players.

Four-wall handball is practically the only game played outside Metropolitan New York City. Every city throughout this country and Canada has one or more four-wall courts available. In YMCA's, YMHA's, and many privates clubs like the Los Angeles A. C., Olympic A. C., St. Paul A. C., Minneapolis A. C., Lake Shore A. C., New York A. C., and many others, four-wall courts are available.

SEMIGLASS COURTS

Four-wall handball is a very scientific game in which skill, timing, speed are essential factors in playing the difficult side, back, and corner wall shots. Spectators enjoy watching these clever shots off the back wall. Unfortunately, with the exception of those sitting in the front row of the gallery, it is impossible to see any back wall and corner play. The further one sits back in the gallery, the less he sees of the court.

Within the past ten years or so spectator participation has been greatly improved by the introduction of a special type of safety glass panels in the construction of new courts and in the remodeling of existing courts. Many courts throughout the country have the back wall all or part glass. Courts where sufficient space is available have the upper part of one or both side walls of glass. The additional gallery space behind the glass panels makes it possible for many spectators to watch and enjoy a good game of handball. They are brought close to the play and can easily follow the ball and watch the skills and techniques of the players when making the back wall shots.

These semiglass courts, three variations of which are shown in the Appendix, pages 81 to 83, are the answer to a greater appreciation of the game. It is our hope that plans for the construction of new four-wall courts and the remodeling of existing courts throughout the country will call for some glass sections or a side wall or/and a back wall. These semiglass courts are a popular innovation, attract many spectators, greatly increase interest of members in handball, result in more members playing—all age groups, and are an incentive in attracting new members and a profitable investment for any club.

HOW THE GAME IS PLAYED

OFFICIAL HANDBALL RULES BOOK

To enjoy playing, and to know what to do or not to do, you should be familiar with the handball rules, at least the fundamental ones concerning serving, receiving, scoring, shorts, and hinders. It would be advisable to secure a copy of the Official Unified Handball Rules Book, which governs all handball games and tournaments. In 1959, a most progressive step was taken in the interest of handball, in its development and popularity, when the AAU, YMCA, USHA, and JWB adopted one set of rules. These Unified Handball Rules are now the official rules for all handball games. Copies of these rules are usually on file in places where handball is played.

The following procedure applies to one-, three-, and four-wall games:

The player who is serving drops the ball to the floor, within the service zone, and on the first rebound it is struck by the hand in such manner that it will first hit the front wall and on the rebound land upon the floor back of the short line in the receiving zone. If the server fails to serve the ball legally as specified in the rules, there is a penalty.

After the ball is legally served, one of the players on the receiving side returns the ball by striking it with his hand, either on the fly or on the first bounce, so that it will strike the front wall before striking the floor and on its rebound from the wall the serving side then returns the ball to the front wall as just stated and play continues until either the serving side or the receiving side is unable to return the ball legally. If the receiving side fails to return the ball legally, it is a point for the serving side. If the serving side fails to return the ball legally, it is a handout.

Only the side serving can score points.

The side first scoring 21 points wins the game.

SINGLES, DOUBLES, "CUT-THROAT"

Handball may be played by two, three, or four people. In *singles* two play one opposing the other. In *doubles* four play—two players on each side. After the first service of each game, when only one handout is the rule, each player of a team serves until both hands are out. The opposing team then serves until both hands are out.

In *"cut-throat"* three play—for example, "A," "B," "C." Assume "A" serves first, he plays against "B" and "C" as a team. When "A" 's hand is put out, "B" plays against "A" and "C" as a team. When "B" 's hand is put out, "C" plays against "A" and "B" as a team and service rotates in like manner. Only the player serving can score points.

PLAYERS' EQUIPMENT

To derive the full benefit of the game, both physical and mental, and to enjoy playing, whether it be four-, three-, or one-wall, your playing equipment should be selected with care.

GLOVES

Rules require that gloves must be worn at all times while the game is in progress. Gloves must be light in color, consisting of soft material or leather. No foreign substance such as tape or rubber bands should be used on the fingers or palms of the gloves. There are handball gloves with a padded playing surface, but these are seldom used; the plain leather type is recommended.

To secure the best results, gloves should fit the hand snugly and should be tightened around the wrist to prevent slipping. Most handball gloves are equipped with drawstrings, which permit tightening the gloves around the wrist. If gloves slip to any extent, rubber bands or adhesive tape should be used to fasten the gloves securely at the wrist. A loose glove, or a glove that slips on the hand, handicaps the player and causes a loss of control as well as speed.

SHOES

The game of handball requires quick starts, stops, and fast footwork. Players should be equipped with the proper type of shoe to avoid slipping, which sometimes is the cause of sprained ankles or other leg injuries.

Players should wear a high-laced shoe of the suction or crepe sole type, similar to those worn by basketball players. A good suction shoe grips the floor, eliminates slipping, and gives the player confidence in quick starts and stops when playing the ball. Shoes should be securely laced to give proper support to the ankles.

Some players are frequently bothered with blistered feet. This is usually caused by the foot slipping within the shoe when the feet start to perspire, causing skin irritation and blisters. As a preventative, heavy woolen socks are recommended. They absorb perspiration, grip the foot snugly, feel comfortable, and will afford the desired relief.

UNIFORM

Rules provide that players are required to wear white suits, shirt, pants, and socks. Sweatshirts and pants are suggested when playing conditions warrant or to work up a good sweat. An athletic supporter should be worn to prevent groin or strain injuries.

STANDARD HANDBALL

By all means start playing with a standard official handball. The official ball is black in color, $1\frac{7}{8}$ inches in diameter, 2.3 ounces in weight: with a rebound from 42 to 48 inches when dropped from a height of 70 inches at a temperature of 68 degrees. These balls can be purchased at any sporting goods store and at YMCA's, YMHA's, and private clubs. Do not start playing with a tennis or any other type of soft ball.

PLAYING CONTRIBUTORS

If this book has any merit at all, and serves its purpose as a guide to beginners, much of the credit is due to the contributions of the following national champions. In my opinion they form the greatest aggregation of players competing in any one era in handball history.

In reading through these pages the suggestions and advice of the contributors, famous players, all holding many national championships, and that of the author may vary a little and possibly be a trifle confusing. This is to be expected as no two champions in any sport play the game exactly alike. To accomplish the same net result they may use different approaches, strategy, body position, etc. However, fundamentally their suggestions and methods on plays will accomplish the same result—just a little difference in execution.

Beginners may follow the advice of one contributor on some particular play and that of another on some other play. Follow the advice that appeals to you as sound and practical and that best fits your style and physical makeup. Your game is bound to improve.

The Obert Brothers. Left to right, Carl, Oscar, and Rubrecht "Ruby" of the New York Athletic Club. These brothers have had a sensational career. Residents of the Bronx in New York City they were found almost every day after school and on Saturdays and Sundays playing handball on the one-wall courts in the playgrounds and parks. They developed rapidly, winning the New York City Park Department Championships, then on to greater honors in district, state, and national competition. Oscar, the oldest, has won many national titles in one-, three-, and four-wall handball. In the year 1961 he held five national titles. It was the first time in history that any player accomplished such a feat. In 1962 Oscar won the National USHA Singles Four-Wall title. In 1963 Oscar won both the USHA One- and Four-Wall Championships and teamed with Ruby copped the one-wall doubles title as well. He won the AAU Four-Wall Singles Championship and again with Ruby won the doubles title. Teamed with Ruby they won the AAU Doubles Championship. This makes a total of six national championships held by Oscar in 1963. This feat has never been equaled in handball history. Ruby held three championships in 1963. The three brothers at the end of 1963 had won a total of fifty-five gold medals in one, three, and four walls in both singles and doubles. Each brother is a national champion in his own right. They are three of the greatest players in the United States and form perhaps the greatest trio of brothers to dominate any sport.

Vic Hershkowitz of the Brooklyn Central YMCA. For nearly 25 years he has been one of the top flight players, winning about thirty national titles in one-, three-, and four-wall handball. He was considered to be one of the best ambidextrous players. Vic was a product of the one-wall courts at the Trinity Club, also played at Brighton Beach and Coney Island in New York. He is an extremely competent instructor in helping young men to learn how to play properly. Vic is considered by many handball fans and officials as the best all-around player in handball history.

Jimmy Jacobs, Los Angeles, Calif., one of the "Greats" of all time. He was the first to hold the "triple crown" in four-wall handball. In 1956 he was the National AAU, YMCA, USHA champion. He is a perfectionist in executing all four-wall shots and holds many national titles. Jimmy has held clinics throughout the country and is in demand as a speaker.

John Sloan, Chicago, Ill. John won his first national title at the age of eighteen. His rise to national rating has been meteoric. By the age of twenty-six (1962) he had accumulated eighteen national titles. His youth, speed, excellent control, and execution of all shots will assure him of top-flight rating for many years. It is a real delight to watch his skillful execution of the more difficult shots.

Phil Collins. The names of Sloan and Collins are synonymous with the great doubles teams of handball history. They were AAU National Doubles Champions for 1956, 1957, 1958, and 1959. They also won many YMCA and USHA titles. Collins possesses keen anticipation, is an exceptionally hard hitter, and is considered to be the best front court player in handball.

2

Fundamentals

CARE OF HANDS

It is common with players new to the game, and even occasionally with experienced players, to find that, when starting to play, their hands sting when striking the ball, although they are wearing gloves. This frequently results in "bone bruises," discolored, as well as swollen hands. It is suggested that, before playing, regardless of the temperature of the courts, the hands be placed in a basin of hot water and kept there for a few minutes. This heats the blood, causing free circulation, and eliminates to a great extent bruises and swellings.

GETTING THE FEEL OF THE BALL

As a beginner, your first efforts should be directed toward getting the "feel" of the standard handball. To do so, stand in the center of the court, assume your natural throwing position, as you would for throwing a baseball. Then throw the ball straight to the front wall and catch it on the first bounce. Pick some spot on the wall and see how close you can come to hitting it. Again, catch the ball on the first bounce. Then, change to another spot on the wall, higher or lower, and see how accurate you are in hitting it. Also, try throwing with different speeds—fast, medium, and slow—watching the bounce of the ball and catching it on the first bounce.

After a while, move nearer to the wall, perhaps just in front of the short line, and repeat throwing the ball and catching it on the bounce. Then move nearer to the back wall, or long line, and do the same thing, hitting the front wall at different heights and speeds. Do not attempt to play the ball—that is, to strike it with your hand—but simply catch it on the first bounce.

All this preliminary work is necessary and very important. It should not take more than 15 or 20 minutes to give you the "feel" of the ball and to get you acquainted with it. This practice of testing the speed, angle, and bounce of the ball should be followed before starting any game, as some handballs are faster and livelier than others.

Vic Hershkowitz says: "Beginners would profit more by experimentation than by trusting to luck. Experiment with serving the ball with the proper stance, the proper stroke and rhythm. Do not try to hit the ball as hard as you can. Work first for control, speed comes later. Ask some experienced player for constructive criticism as you serve and play the ball."

HANDBALL STROKES

There are three "must" strokes in handball on which the beginner must concentrate in developing his game, namely: the Underhand, the Sidearm, and Overhand, using both the right and left hands.

Some years ago, when the courts were larger than those of today, the underhand stroke was used rather exclusively. Then, when new courts were built and space was a factor, the courts became smaller in size. This fact, coupled with the manufacture of a faster and livelier ball, caused the sidearm stroke to put in an appearance, which permitted the player to strike the ball quicker, faster, and harder than when using the underhand stroke. Today, the sidearm stroke is very popular and used by all top-flight players.

UNDERHAND STROKE

The proper position for the underhand stroke is to stand sideways to the front wall, a position similar to that of a batter in baseball facing the pitcher. The feet should be spaced comfortably apart, with the left foot toward the wall, the knees bent slightly. The player should time the bounce of the ball so that it will rebound close to the body. The underhand stroke is made by keeping the arm close to the body, shoulders and head bent slight forward, the right shoulder slightly raised. On the start of the upward swing, the weight is shifted to the right leg, with the elbow bent slightly and the right shoulder raised. The arm at the top of the swing is usually at a straight line backward from the shoulder. On the downward swing the arm is still kept close to the body. As the body pivots, the elbow is bent slightly, the hand is cupped, the weight is shifted to the left leg, and the ball is hit at the instant of the upward swing of the arm. The power and force of the stroke is in the forearm and the wrist. The underhand stroke is similar to the motion of the softball pitcher. While practicing this underhand stroke, the beginner should strive for the proper coordination and timing. As your control of the shot increases, move your left foot a step or two forward on the downward swing and pivot for additional power. The stroke is used frequently in serving, particularly for the "hook" ball, and when playing backwall shots in four-wall.

Ruby Obert shown about to strike the ball with an underhand swing. Body just slightly bent; arm, on its downward motion, will be close to the body when striking the ball, using a full underhand motion.

Vic Hershkowitz showing how to use the side arm swing. Notice body well bent over, arm sharply bent at elbow and well away from the body, left foot firmly on the floor, ball is struck with a side arm motion, all power in the stroke coming from the forearm and wrist.

1   2

Sequence A.   Side Arm Stroke.

5

Sequence A. Sidearm Stroke.   You can quickly improve your sidearm stroke by closely following the start and completion of this stroke as shown in Sequence A. Here Oscar Obert (1) is in position to play the ball, weight on his right foot, eye on the ball. As the ball approaches him (2) arm is bent at elbow, hand cupped, weight shifting slightly to his left foot as he starts his body pivot and gets set to strike the ball. (3) and (4) show the ball about to be struck and in (5) the ball can be seen after being struck. (6) and (7) show the body pivot completed, weight on the left leg in an excellent follow through position. For those who are interested in practicing "kill" shots Sequence A could be very helpful, as the player is in the proper position, body well bent over, to play for a "kill."

3   4

6   7

SIDEARM STROKE

The proper stance for the sidearm stroke, as far as the body and feet are concerned, is about the same as that used for the underhand stroke. The body, however, is bent forward to a greater degree. The feet are well balanced, with the knees bent slightly, and the bounce of the ball is so timed that it will bounce about twelve to fifteen inches away from the player, depending on the height of the player. At the upward sidearm motion of the arm the body pivots, the right shoulder drops slightly, and the height and upward swing of the arm are about even with the shoulder.

1   2

Sequence B.   Overhand Shot.

5

Sequence B. Overhand Shot.   In this sequence Carl Obert is getting set to play an overhand shot. The position of his feet and body indicates that his purpose is to play the ball so that it will first strike the left side of the front wall. A slightly different position is taken if the ball will first strike the right side of the front wall.

As the ball approaches Carl (1 and 2) his weight is on the right foot, arm raised with elbow bent, hand cupped, eye on the ball. As the ball gets closer, arm is raised to meet the ball and the ball is just being struck by the hand, arm

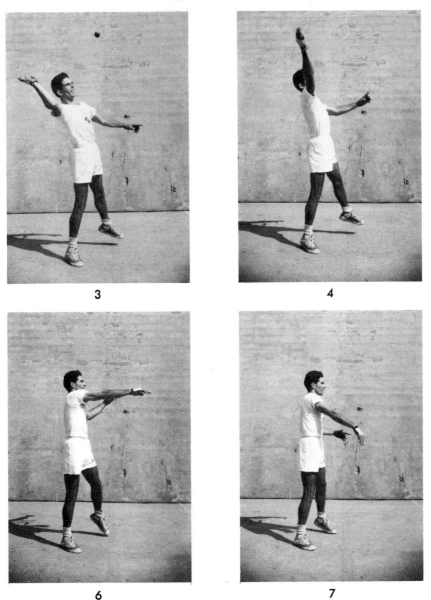

3   4

6   7

Sequence B.   Overhand Shot. *Continued.*

is straight up, weight on right foot (4). As the ball is on its way to the front wall (5), body starts pivoting and the follow through is completed (7).

Although these pictures show the position and stroke used on a descending ball, practically the same position and stroke are used when the player strikes the ball on its rise from the floor. In single-wall more than in four-wall the overhand stroke is used when playing high bouncing balls on the rise. In single-wall the player frequently steps in and uses the overhand stroke in striking the ball on its rise.

On the downward swing, the arm is extended about ten to fifteen inches away from the body, the elbow is bent, the hand is cupped and, as the body pivots, the hand hits the ball with a sidearm motion, the weight shifting to the left foot. Most of the power and drive of the sidearm shot is in the forearm and wrist. The arc of the swing is shorter and wider (away from the body) than the underhand stroke.

OVERHAND STROKE

In a good fast game a player is frequently called upon to use an overhand stroke. For high bounding balls, playing balls on the fly, or to force an opponent out of position, a good overhand stroke is a strong weapon. It is primarily a defensive shot, to keep the ball in play. But, for players who can control it, the overhand is a strong offensive shot for passing purposes. It is also very effective when making a "lob" serve.

For an overhand right-handed stroke, approximately three quarters of the body should be facing the front wall with the left foot extended forward and sideways to the left. The body is kept erect, with the head and shoulders bent slightly backward. The arm is raised above the head to a height

Jimmy Jacobs shows how to play an overhand shot. Body well balanced, left foot firmly on the floor, eye on the ball, elbow bent slightly, hand slightly cupped, ball is struck with the power coming from the forearm and wrist.

depending on the bounce of the ball. If the height permits, for speed and/or control, bend the elbow, cup the hand, and strike the ball with a semi-sidearm motion, pivoting the body as you follow through with the arm. A very fast and controlled ball can be delivered with this stroke. If the ball that you are playing should bounce high, a straight arm and an open hand should be used. A player will have many occasions to use the overhand stroke. Practice timing, balance, and control.

STRAIGHT ARM

This is a stroke that the average player uses for defense purposes and, most always, with the weak hand. However, it is used offensively only by a few of the more experienced players. As its name implies, it is a straight arm open hand shot and is made with a full sweeping follow-through motion of the arm. It is used in many cases to bring the ball straight off the front wall, or as a cross-court play, or passing shot, depending on the position of the opponent and the skill of the player in making the shot.

Jimmy Jacobs says: "Do not be too ambitious in the beginning and use all the power you have in striking the ball. Start slowly. Keep your eye on the ball. Practice playing the ball off the front wall on the first bounce, from different positions on the floor. Concentrate on control and direction, using both right and left hand. As you gain confidence, and your control improves, put a little more power into your shots."

PLAYING THE BALL

Your next step in fundamentals is to play the ball—that is, to strike it on its first bounce. There is no better way to practice this return play than to stand in the middle of the court about the short line. Bounce the ball, hit it to the front wall, and on the first bounce return it to the front wall. Do not try to "kill" it or hit it as hard as you can. When the ball is on its way to the front wall, try to anticipate from its speed or height about where it will strike the floor on its return and the bounce that it will take. Immediately start for the anticipated spot and get into position to play the return. Simply try to hit the ball to the front wall and, on its return, hit it again to the front wall. See how many times you can return the ball on its first bounce, keeping it in play without missing.

When a ball is on its way to the front wall, think and act like an outfielder in baseball, who starts running at the crack of the bat to get into position to play the ball.

After you have played the ball from the short line, move back about five to ten feet and repeat the procedure. This distance will require more power, speed, and control. Then move further back and do the same thing.

Have patience; do not be too anxious to start playing until you have more confidence. If you do play a game, your opponent should be someone who is just a little more advanced than you. Learn from your own mistakes and your opponent's; watch how he plays the ball; observe his stance, his balance, the strokes he uses, the way he covers the court.

Oscar Obert says: "Beginners are frequently advised to practice hitting the ball to the front wall at different angles and speeds, to get the feel of the ball. That is good advice and should be followed, but only to a certain extent. In my opinion, fifteen minutes or so of individual instruction by an experienced player, showing how to cup the hand, bounce the ball, to take position when playing different shots, will benefit a new player more than trying to learn these shots by himself."

Now that you have acquired the "feel" of the ball and are somewhat familiar with its speed and bounce, let us proceed with suggestions as to how to strike the ball.

The rules of handball provide that "only one hand at any one time may be used in hitting the ball." So, if the ball is returned by the wrist or forearm, the player is penalized by a point or handout, as the case may be.

For all instructional purposes and simplicity, we shall assume that the player is right-handed. For a left-handed player the reverse would be true.

EYE ON THE BALL

As is common with many sports a cardinal rule in handball is "keep your eye on the ball."

This is particularly true as the handball is black in color, small in size, and only 1⅞ inches in diameter. When serving don't take your eye off the ball. While the ball is in play follow its flight carefully; keep your eyes on it while moving into position to play it and right up to the time the hand meets the ball.

Many handball players, as in golf and tennis, look away as they are about to hit the ball. This many times results in a poor shot—the ball is not struck properly and may glance off the hand. Try to remember that the walls are always there, they won't move. Don't, as you are about to strike the ball, look in the direction you plan to hit it. Concentrate on keeping your eye on the ball until the impact of hand and ball is made.

STANCE

In serving and playing the ball, the stance is very important: Be comfortable, perfectly balanced. There is not just one stance to use. Baseball players, while at bat, have different positions and stances. Some crowd the plate, others stand farther back, some with feet close together, others with feet spread apart, some bent forward, others standing erect. This is also true of handball players. No two players stand exactly alike. Just be comfortable and at ease, swing and pivot easily.

Let us start with the easiest of all balls to hit—the ball you bounce on the floor and strike on its rebound. Stand at the short line, take a comfortable position with your left side toward the front wall, knees slightly bent, feet spread apart so that you are well balanced with the shoulders and head bent slightly forward. Most right-handed players on service drop the ball with their left hand so that the rebound will be 12 to 15 inches high. As the ball is dropped, shift your weight to your right leg, raise your arm, bent at the elbow, with the hand slightly cupped. As the ball rebounds to the proper height and the body pivots, the downward or sidearm swing of the arm must be timed so that the hand, moving at its greatest speed, will meet the ball fully and properly to propel it to the front wall.

In serving, many experienced players take a step forward with their left foot toward the front wall when striking the ball. The purpose is to get more body into the stroke, more power. This step forward requires more control and precision than when the player stands with both feet on the floor spread about 12 to 15 inches apart. We suggest that in serving the beginner stand with both feet spread apart. This affords more control, easier pivoting, and follow-through. A most important factor in serving is to see that you are not off balance when you complete the stroke, as you should quickly get into position to play your opponent's return.

Carl Obert says: "When I started playing one-wall handball I had the advantage of my brother Oscar's experience. He showed me how to hit the ball properly, using the forearm power, how to pivot, and he drilled me on control, because control is the most important factor in one-wall. My advice to beginners is to do as I did. Ask some experienced player to give you fifteen minutes or so of instruction on how to make the different shots."

TIMING

Timing in handball, as in every sport, is essential for speed and control. As a beginner just try to hit the ball so that it will strike the front wall about where you want it to. Time the impact of hand and ball so that the result will give you the speed, direction, or control you are aiming for. Practice diligently in timing your stroke so that it will be at its greatest force with the impact of the ball and hand. Proper timing, as I said, is not confined to speed and force alone. It is required for soft lob plays, also in slow passing shots and ceiling shots. Proper timing and coordination will add materially to your game. However, it comes with practice— a lot of practice.

WEAK HAND

To be a competent ambidextrous player is the ambition of every handball player. If you aspire to a club championship, or even a Class "A" or "B" rating, your success will depend to a great extent on your ability to play the ball effectively with right or left hand. Developing your weak

Illustrating awkward position of player using his right hand to play a ball that is close to the left side wall. He is completely off balance. His return shot will be a weak one if it reaches the front wall at all. Player is out of position and his opponent will have an open court in which to return the ball. This picture clearly illustrates the necessity of developing your weak hand.

hand automatically strengthens your arm, shoulder, and leg muscles. It saves many steps and energy, but like everything else, requires practice and concentration.

A player with a weak hand is soon spotted and his opponents quickly take advantage of it. At every opportunity they will direct their attacks against the weak hand.

Beginners, and even many advanced players, will return every ball possible with their strong hand. A strong right-handed player will run to the left side of the court to return a ball with his right hand. This handicaps the player, as he is off balance and usually out of position for the return play.

If your left hand is the weak one, here is a suggestion. Try throwing the ball to the front wall with your left hand and catching on the first bounce with your left hand. Then practice hitting the ball on the first bounce at different distances from the wall. The position of your feet is very important: feel comfortable, use follow-through, body-pivot motion.

You can improve your left hand by playing a game with an opponent who is about equal to you in ability, both of you using only the left hand in serving and returning the ball. This will not only improve the weak hand, but provide an interesting game. Since one seldom uses his weak hand, you will find it awkward to strike the ball with any degree of speed or control at first. But do not get discouraged; keep trying. Another suggestion is that, during a game, you serve occasionally with your left hand.

You may lose the game, but you will profit by the experience and win many other games.

If you are a right-handed player, all balls close to the left line or side-wall should be played with the left hand. As a beginner, do not try to kill or use a passing shot with your weak hand, as the percentage of success is against you. In most cases your weak hand should be used for defensive purposes.

If you play four-wall handball, where control is not as important a factor as in one-wall, and you have more confidence and balance, try striking the ball with the weak hand using a "fist" or punch return. This propels the ball with greater force than when struck by the open hand.

In any game, balls going sharply to your left should be returned by your left hand. However, if you can return some of these left-side balls with your right hand without sacrificing position, do so. Do not sacrifice force, control, and position by using your weak hand if your strong hand can easily make the play.

FLY BALL

A fly ball is one that you strike before the ball hits the floor. To be effective with this shot requires a lot of practice and proper timing. If you have had some baseball experience, hitting these fly balls will not be too much of a problem. The thing is to know which balls to hit on the fly and which ones to let bounce.

The use of the fly-ball return depends to a great extent on the court

Jimmy Jacobs getting set to return the ball on the fly. Notice eye on the ball, arm bent at elbow, right foot firmly on the floor, body well balanced. Carl Obert watching to see direction of Jimmy's return shot. This is a good action picture.

position of your opponent and on your position as well. It can be used as a kill, a passing, or a ceiling shot. If you are up front and your opponent is in the back court, a fly kill could be attempted. If you are in the back court and your opponent is up front, a fly ball should be played to force your opponent to the back court and out of position. Occasionally, the return of a ball on the fly will catch your opponent off guard, since he may not expect it, which is to your advantage.

The best position at which to play fly balls is in the center of the court around the short line. The ball has to be hit quickly, using the right or left hand as needed. But a fly ball should be played only if you are set for it and it is an easy return. If you are out of position, off balance, or have to lunge for the fly ball, do not attempt it. Let it take its bounce and then play it.

A service ball may be returned on the fly, but a receiver is not permitted to run in over the short line to play it.

HOOK SERVE

It is the ambition of nearly all beginners, after they have seen an experienced player serving a hook ball, immediately to try to emulate him. As this hook serve is without doubt the most difficult to master, leave it alone for the time being. It should be attempted only after a player has acquired the skills necessary for control and accuracy in using the underhand, sidearm, and overhand strokes. Very few top-flight players have developed the hook serve to the extent that they can use it effectively and consistently.

The purpose of the hook serve is to cause the ball to break sharply to the right or left on striking the floor. This sharp break usually puts the receiver off balance, preventing him from returning the ball with any degree of accuracy or speed. In some cases, because of the sharp break, the ball completely eludes the receiver.

Only fair speed is required to serve hook balls. The most important factor is the timing of the motion of the hand as it meets the ball. In attempting a hook serve, assuming that the player is right-handed, he should

x   y

"Hook" serves.

Vic Hershkowitz starting to serve a "hook" ball shows position of cupped hand, ball being struck by the lower part of the palm and the small finger with an upward and overhand swing so that the spin of the ball when striking the floor will cause it to hook to the right side of the court.

stand facing the right side of the court, with the left side of the body toward the front wall. The server's hand should be slightly cupped, with the thumb held close to the first or index finger and the palm turned slightly upward. In serving a ball that breaks sharply to the left after striking the floor, the motion is a sort of underhand slice, so that the ball, when struck, will spin off the palm and the thumb causing the ball to break to the left on striking the floor, as shown in the illustration (marked X).

To serve a hook ball that breaks sharply to the right after striking the floor, it is necessary to develop a stroke directly opposite to that used for the left hook. The ball must be struck with an overhand motion, that is, drawn across the ball, so that the ball will spin off the base of the hand and the little finger as shown in the illustration (Y).

Carl Obert has exceptionally sharp breaking "hook" serves. Here is what he says: "The hook serve should not be attempted by beginners. It takes a lot of practice, timing, and patience, before one masters it to any extent. Many top-flight players have never been too successful with it. However, here is how I serve the hook ball: If the ball is to hit to the right of the receiver, it should be struck with a slightly cupped hand, the thumb

Vic Hershkowitz about to serve a hook ball showing position of cupped hand—ball being struck by the palm close to the thumb in an underhand slicing swing so that the returned ball when striking the floor will hook to the left side of the court.

close to the index finger, with an underhand slicing motion. The ball spins off the thumb and upper part of the palm and, after striking the floor, hooks to the right side of the player. For the ball to hook to the left of the player, the ball is struck by the lower part of the cupped hand in an upward and overhand motion. As the ball strikes the floor it hooks to the left."

PUNCH BALL

The "punch" or fist ball is used by practically every advanced player offensively, and in many cases defensively. For the average player, however, it is confined to defensive use. Since the beginner is most interested in control, the use of the slightly cupped open hand is better for him. The punch ball is used by four-wall players more than by those who play one-wall, because the four-wall player has four walls and a ceiling to help his control, while the one-wall player requires a greater degree of control and accuracy, because of the open sides and the back line.

For those who desire to use the punch ball stroke, or to improve their ability to use it, the following advice may help.

Position of hand for the "fist" stroke.

The fingers are closed across the palm of the hand in the form of a fist, with the thumb extending over the index finger (see illustration above). The same underhand or sidearm motion is used as in striking the ball with the palm of the hand, but now the object is to strike the ball with the knuckles. The hard bony surface of the fist propels the ball with considerably more speed than if struck with the open hand. Frequently the ball may be struck with the heel of the hand, which also results in an exceptionally speedy ball. The purpose of the punch ball is to return the ball with such speed that it hurries the opponent and prevents him from

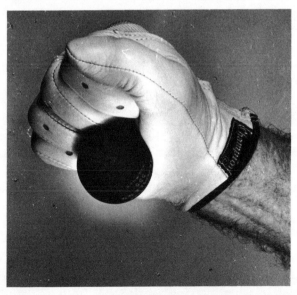

Here is a good close-up shot of a fist ball showing how the ball should be struck with the fingers and heel of the hand.

Ruby Obert showing the position of the body, well balanced, arm bent when using the first shot on a low ball.

getting into position for a good return. It is also effective when used as a passing shot, provided the player can control the ball.

For beginners the punch ball, however, is very difficult to control, especially as to direction, because of the small hitting area of the fist. It is effective when playing the ball with the weak hand, since the bony surface gives the ball greater speed than when struck by the open hand. A good defensive fist shot with the weak hand results in less setups for opponents and improves your game.

Johnny Sloan says: "Beginners should first become proficient using the open or cupped hand return before attempting to use the fist shot. However, it should be practiced and occasionally used, particularly when a good opportunity presents itself. Due to the small hitting area of the fist you have less control than when using the open hand. The fist ball is used by most players as a defensive shot where control is not too much of a factor."

Ruby Obert says: "A well-controlled fist ball helps a great deal. If properly hit, the ball has greater speed than when hit with the open hand. It is used very often when playing a ball with the weak hand because of its greater speed. It is used for passing and ceiling shots and for forcing players away from the front court."

BACKSWING

We all like to hit the ball as hard as we can and this is particularly true of the average player when competing in tournaments with spectators present. The average player, more than a topflight player, likes to impress spectators with his hard hit speedy balls. This greater power and speed of the ball is sometimes attempted by taking a long high back swing, the theory being that the higher the backswing, the faster the downward swing, and the greater the power and speed of the ball. This theory is not always true, particularly for the average player who is very apt to strive too hard, lose control, timing, and follow through on the downward swing, and wind up being off balance after striking the ball. He often dissipates his power completely.

I am reminded of a fine young player who was making excellent progress, won a class "B" tournament, and could hold his own with many class "A" fellows. He had speed, good control, and deception. However, when he entered a class "A" tournament he was usually eliminated quickly. It was noticed that in tournament play he wanted to show class "A" players how hard he could hit the ball, the great speed of the ball. His windup was high and exaggerated, his downward swing very fast, his purpose was just to hit the ball as hard and as fast as he could. By doing this he sacrificed timing, control, and direction and was making many weak returns. When this fault was called to his attention and he corrected it, he quickly improved his game and is now one of our really topflight players.

FOOTWORK

In most athletic games footwork is a most important factor. Handball is a very fast game—quick starts, stops, speeds, etc. Footwork has a dual purpose—first, to get you there and second, to be in a position to make an effective shot.

While serving, you have the opportunity to get set for your serve—feet properly placed, comfortable body position, and easy pivot. However, while the ball is in play and traveling around the court pretty fast, you may not have the opportunity to get set for your return shot. You may have but a second or two to get into position to play the ball. The effectiveness of your return shot as to speed and direction of the ball may depend a great deal on the position of your feet, and on body motion when striking the ball.

In planning your return shots give as much or more thought to the position of your feet when striking the ball as you do to getting to the ball to play it. If and when you get to the ball you are off balance, your shot is apt to be a poor one. If possible time your approach to the ball so that when you strike it you will be on the balls of your feet evenly balanced and not on your toes or heels.

Many hard-hit balls will land at your feet, not permitting you to get set for a return play. These balls require a quick scoop shot. Other fast-hit balls will come directly at you on the fly requiring a push shot that is pushing the ball away from you. The scoop and push shots are for defensive purposes; you usually are off balance and your play is simply to get the ball back to the front wall.

Gus Lewis, a former champion noted for his easy body movement and position in making his shots, says "just DRIFT and not run to the anticipated spot to return the ball."

Some few years ago a player with excellent control and power, when he could get set for the ball, was not effective at all when he had to quickly move into position to play the ball. His fault was that when playing balls that required quick movement to get into position for his shot he would *dash* to the spot where he wanted to play the ball and as a result he frequently overran the ball, had to check himself sharply, step back, and was not in a good position to play the ball. When this was called to his attention and he became a "drifter," his game improved.

BODY POSITION

An ambitious young fellow playing about three months who could hit the ball pretty well and had good speed became rather disappointed at the slow progress he was making in properly playing the balls he could get set for. Although he had no trouble in hitting the ball, he could, as they say "do nothing with it." He asked his friend the club champion what he was doing wrong. After closely watching his play his friend detected a fault that is somewhat common with beginners and that is in practically every low shot—he, a right-handed player, was striking the ball as it came off the floor close to his left foot. In others words, the ball was "in front" of him. This resulted in his striking the ball on the upward swing of the arm. In so doing he was off balance, more on his toes than on the balls of his feet, he had to push his head forward a little, his control and timing were bad, and while he could get the ball back to the front wall, he "had nothing on it." It was an easy return play for his opponent.

When this fault was pointed out to him, he quickly made the proper adjustment in his body position so that the ball off the floor came to him a little closer to his right foot. He felt comfortable, properly balanced, and his head was directly over the ball, which was struck the instant the downward swing—or the side arm swing, as the case may be—reached its lowest point and the swing started its upward motion. He got the full power of the shot, his control and timing were much better, and his game quickly improved—so did his morale.

The reverse of this "off the left foot shot" is found when you play balls that come off the right foot, the ball being "in back" of you—both result in poor returns. The more experienced tournament players occasionally play a ball that comes off their left foot. This is attempted when playing a soft passing or kill shot, particularly when the opponent is out of position.

For a high lob return shot, striking the ball as it comes slightly off your left foot is proper as you strike the ball with the upward swing of the arm.

However, as a beginner your overall game, particularly when playing low shots, will greatly improve if you make sure the ball comes off the floor evenly between the spread of your feet, your head directly over the ball and your swing timed to hit the ball the instant the swing has reached its lowest point. This will give you a natural pivot and follow-through motion of the arm.

COURT CONDUCT

As a beginner, practically all of your playing will be in just pickup games, probably played without the services of a referee. Because of this, you and your opponent should be somewhat familiar with the playing rules: service, shorts, and particularly hinders, which are covered in another chapter. A knowledge of the principal rules and their proper application will help to assure a friendly atmosphere and an enjoyable game.

Do not serve the ball until your opponent or opponents are in proper position to receive your service.

Give your opponent a fair chance to return the ball. After you have served the ball, and also while the ball is in play, do not cross in front of the ball to get into position to return your opponent's shot. If your opponent is playing the shot, do not crowd or push him; do not stand in his way so that you prevent him from seeing the ball. In four-wall it is your duty after playing the ball to get out of the way of your opponent.

On questionable plays, if you believe you struck the ball on the second bounce, say so. If a ball strikes your wrist or forearm in making a shot and then proceeds to the front wall, say so.

When a rally is completed and you are returning the ball to your opponent to serve, bounce the ball to him, do not throw it. Many injuries have resulted from balls being thrown to servers. Bounce it at all times.

Do not argue at length as to whether or not a ball was good or bad, whether you have 16 points and not 15, and so forth. As a beginner you are playing to improve your game and ability; you are looking for fun and good physical exercise. These things are much more important than winning or losing a point. By accepting your opponent's decision on some questionable point or play you impress him with your fairness and sportsmanship, and as a result he reciprocates and the game continues smoothly.

"Do unto others as you would have others do unto you" is a good proverb to follow. It pays dividends.

Do not serve a ball if it is wet from perspiration or because it has come into contact with sweaty clothes. A partially wet ball skids when hitting

Vic Hershkowitz (front) and Carl Obert posing to illustrate a hinder ball. Carl cannot see the ball to play it as Vic is obstructing his view. Under four-wall rules this would be a hinder. Under one-wall rules, as Vic is standing perfectly still, not bending his body in any way to obstruct Carl's view, it would not be a hinder. One of the few instances where one- and four-wall rules differ.

a wall or the floor, and you are taking an unfair advantage of your opponent.

Many rules are accepted rather than printed, such as the rules for good sportsmanship, conduct, etc. Handball is a game, particularly in doubles, where players are close together, moving most of the time, getting into position. Give your opponents a fair shot at the ball. It is not a game of crowding, interference, and shoving, and such action is not in keeping with the purpose and spirit of the game. If this approach is carried out, you will enjoy playing and never be without playing partners.

SUGGESTIONS TO INSTRUCTORS

To increase interest in handball, develop beginners and permit new players to get acquainted and compete with each other, set aside one or two hours a week on designated days for handball instruction.

Individual instruction is very helpful as the novice appreciates the personal attention he is receiving and the corrective suggestions to improve his most glaring weaknesses. Players have different physiques, body movements—"eager beaver" types, etc. Some adapt themselves more quickly than others. If, however, because of number and time, group instruction is necessary, attempt to keep the group to not more than four and if possible consisting of those players about equal in ability. In groups where some players are a little more advanced than others time is wasted in attempting to permit the less experienced players to catch up.

Experience has taught the author first to discuss with beginners the elementary rules, cupped hand, first bounce, hitting the ball, serving, short line, etc. When instructing, of most importance is the proper stance, position of body, free arm motion, proper pivot shifting of weight from one leg to the other, and the follow-through. Practice the body motion and pivot without striking the ball. Of almost equal importance is proper timing and coordination of swing and contact with the ball.

Don't just tell the novice what to do, show him—be patient.

Beginners have different arm motions that need correction. The speed of the ball is developed principally by the power of the forearm, which is bent slightly at the elbow and brings the wrist into play when striking the ball. When a beginner learns how to stroke the ball with some degree or rhythm, forearm power, and speed, he gains confidence and then quickly advances in other developments, control, direction, weak hand improvement, and offensive and defensive play.

The next step is for players about equal in ability to play a game of singles, say for 15 points with an instructor as referee stopping the game when necessary to call attention to the more glaring misplays. Divide players into groups based on their ability and have a round robin of say four players, a 15-point game with the instructor or some experienced player as referee who will comment on the weakness of each player and offer corrective suggestions. Another help is to have these players sit in the gallery with the instructor and watch experienced players in action, paying particular attention to stance, arm motion, stroking the ball, body position, and pivot.

Start a "Ladder" tournament limited to beginners for not more than six players—one game of 25 points. This results in the players making appointments with each other, enjoying playing together, improving about the same pace, and looking forward to playing regularly. After this they should be on their own, playing with more experienced players.

MERITS OF ONE- AND FOUR-WALL GAMES

When an attempt is made to compare the relative merits of one- and four-wall handball games, a very animated discussion surely results.

Four-wall players say that their game requires greater speed, energy, and accuracy than one-wall. It is also a more scientific game because playing the ball off the side and back walls, as well as the ceiling, requires more skill than any play in one-wall. In four-wall, because of the assistance of the side and back walls, the ball is in play longer, necessitating a greater expenditure of energy. Passing and corner kill shots take a greater degree of accuracy and control than in one-wall. Four-wall players derive more enjoyment and pleasure from a game of handball than would be obtained by playing one-wall.

One-wall players are equally insistent that their game requires greater energy because it is much faster. Better physical condition is necessary, because they have to go and get the passing and angle shots, while four-wall players have the assistance of the side and back walls. Greater accuracy is required in one-wall, because the ball must be kept within the side and the long lines. In four-wall, all the balls that strike the side wall and the ceiling would be outside balls in one-wall.

Both exponents have points here. Defensive control in one-wall is a greater factor than in four-wall. A one-wall player must concentrate on keeping the ball within the side and the long lines. A four-wall player is not troubled too much with this mental hazard. However, many offensive shots in four-wall need finer control because the ball may bounce off a side or back wall and may easily change a tough shot into a setup.

Many one-wall players, because of better defensive control and accuracy, have gone on to win four-wall championships. A four-wall player, attempting one-wall, has a difficult time in adjusting his play, particularly on his defensive returns to keep the ball in fair territory. Very few, if any, four-wall champions, after trying one-wall, ever won a one-wall championship.

3

Four-Wall Handball

STANDARD SIZE COURT

Standard specifications of a four-wall court are:

The court shall be: 20 feet wide
20 feet high
40 feet long
Back wall: 12 feet high

Short Line. The court shall be divided into a front and back court of equal dimensions by a line called the *short line* running parallel with the front wall.

Service Line. Five feet in front of the short line there shall be another parallel line called the *service line*. The space between the outer edges of these two lines shall be known as the *service zone*.

Service Box. Eighteen inches from and parallel with each side wall a line shall be drawn to form a box, termed the *service box,* where the partner of the server in doubles shall stand with his back to the side wall, both feet on the ground.

All lines shall be 1½ inches wide.

Position of Players. In singles server must stand and complete his service within the service zone, shown in drawing. Receiver must stand in the receiving zone (which is the area between the short line and the back wall) and at least five feet back of the short line while the ball is being served.

In doubles server must start and complete his serve within the serving zone. Partner must stand in the service box while the ball is being served.

Receiving side must stand in the receiving zone at least five feet back of the short line while the ball is being served.

ANGLES

Four-wall is a very scientific, popular, and interesting game. In addition to providing splendid physical exercise, it also requires a degree of mental

37

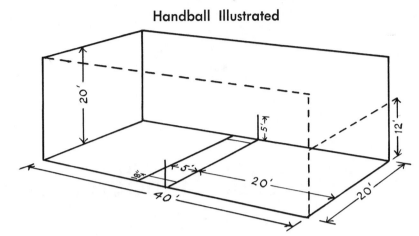

The dimensions of a standard four-wall court.

activity and timing to anticipate quickly where the ball will strike the floor so that a good return shot may be made.

A four-wall court is like a billiard table. To be successful at billiards one has to be thoroughly familiar with the many angles that the ball takes off the cushions as well as the proper control, speed, and direction. The same applies to four-wall handball.

As a beginner, let us assume that you have the "feel" of the ball as suggested on page 13. Your job now is to familiarize yourself with the angles of the ball as it comes off the side and back walls. Start throwing the ball around the court so that it will first strike the front wall, then a side wall, and then the floor. Study carefully the angles taken by the ball as it comes off the side wall and back walls. Keep your eyes on the ball, try to anticipate approximately where it will strike the floor, and move to catch it on the

Proper position of players in a four-wall court. Ready to serve is Oscar Obert, standing between the service and short line. His partner, Carl Obert, is standing with both feet in the service box, back against the wall. Ruby Obert (left) and Vic Hershkowitz are in back court approximately three to four feet in front of backwall set to play served ball.

first bounce. The common expression is: "Let the ball come to you. Don't chase after it."

Alternate throwing the ball at the side wall, left wall, and right wall, at different heights and speeds, and from different positions on the floor. The more you practice angle shots the less trouble you will have in playing them.

HOW TO SERVE

Serving is the most important factor in handball.

More study and concentration should be devoted to acquiring an effective service than to any other phase of playing techniques. You score points only on your serve and consequently your service should be made with precision, control, and deception. The objective of serving is to deliver an ace ball, or at least not to give your opponent a "setup" or an easy serve to return.

There is no one serve that stands out above all others—no cure-all serve. Good players, as a rule, have an assortment of serves that they use during a game. They frequently employ a direct change of pace—that is, from a very fast cross serve to a lob, or a scotch serve. A server is somewhat like a baseball pitcher who, to be effective, must have a good assortment of pitches; fast ball, curve, slider, and letup. The pitcher attempts to out-guess the batter; the batter tries to outguess the pitcher. It is a battle of wits. If the pitcher has only one good pitch, say a fast ball, and throws it consistently, the batter knows what to expect, gets set for it, and has little trouble with it. The same principle applies in handball. Mix up your serves, keep your opponent guessing and off balance.

Every player should develop at least one good effective serve that should be used more than any other—in other words, his "bread and butter" serve.

The server may start serving from any place in the service zone or area. As a rule, the server stands in the center of the serving area so that he can serve either to right or left and be in a good position to play his opponent's return shot.

Know what is a good serve and what is not. Any two illegal serves in succession put the server out. Illegal serves are listed in the Sypnosis of Unified Four-Wall Rules on page 77.

Care should be taken not to put your hand out by a served ball. If the served ball hits the ceiling, floor, or side wall before striking the front wall your hand is out.

Jimmy Jacobs says: "Frequently change the spot in the court where your served ball will land and frequently change the speed of the ball. If you consistently serve a ball with the same speed a receiver knows what to expect, even though the served ball may be directed to different parts of the court. If you change your speed the receiver must adjust his timing and position."

One of the cardinal rules of handball is to study your opponent's game and play to his weakness.

LOB, CROSS COURT, SCOTCH SERVES

A description of different types of served balls follows:

(a) Low fast sharp angle serve. The ball strikes the floor back of the short line and rebounds sharply to a side wall.

(b) Low fast ball, sharp angle, first striking a side wall and then the floor back of the short line.

(c) Low fast angle ball that, on its rebound from the floor, strikes a side wall, then the back wall.

(d) A low fast straight ball that strikes the floor back of the short line and hugs the side wall.

(e) Lob serve—ball striking high on the front wall close to the side wall, striking the floor just over the short line, then rebounding high so that it slides down the side wall into the corner as shown below.

(f) Scotch toss serve. The server stands close to the wall, say on the right side, and serves the ball with sufficient speed so that it will hit high on the front wall then hit the left side wall, then strike the floor a few feet back of the short line and, on its rebound, hit the back and right side wall, or the right side wall and then the back. The object is to have the ball come off the wall as close to the wall as possible. This Scotch serve is also very effective when the ball is hit hard and properly controlled.

There is also the "hook" serve that should be used only by the more experienced players. A description and the purpose of the hook serve are shown on page 26.

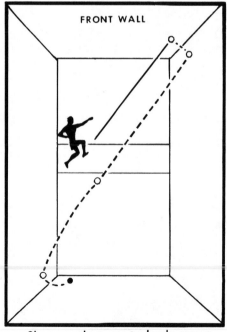

Sharp angle serve to back corner.

High side wall lob serve.

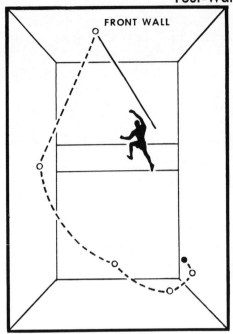

Scotch serve.

"Hopping" the ball right and left.

In delivering low fast angle serves an effort should be made to hit the "crack" that, in handball parlance, is the junction of the floor and the side wall. In such cases, the ball usually takes a bad bounce, eludes the receiver, or results in a weak return. The law of averages will give you many points by hitting the "crack."

Oscar Obert says: "The most important part of the game is serving the ball. You have the advantage over your opponent, so keep him guessing. Most top-flight players have at least one effective serve. It scores points or results in weak returns. Develop a serve which you like. Work on it, but do not use it for every serve. Mix them up."

The serve should be used to get as many points, or aces, as possible. Try not to give your opponent an easy serve. A served ball that goes straight down the center of the court and comes off the back wall is an easy ball to return and, to many players, is a "setup" for a kill or a passing shot.

A good effective serve usually results in an ace or a weak return, giving the server an opportunity for a kill or a passing shot.

RECEIVER

Handball rules require that the receiver must stand at least five feet back of the short line while the ball is being served. The rules also provide that a receiver is permitted to play a legal service either on the fly—that is, before it strikes the floor, or on the first bounce. A receiver is not permitted to run in over the short line to play a served ball on the fly.

In four-wall handball the receiver should take a position approximately three to five feet in front of the back wall and about the center of the court.

If you are a right-handed player and your left hand is rather weak, your position should be a foot or two nearer the left side wall. Your body position should be somewhat like that of an infielder in baseball, feet spread apart and the body well balanced. There should be more pressure on the balls of the feet with the body bent forward slightly, knees flexed so that you are ready to take off as soon as the ball is struck by the server. From the speed, height, and direction of the served ball try immediately to approximate where the ball will strike the floor or wall and move quickly into the proper position to play it. As you move toward the ball, decide how you will return the ball—that is, a kill, passing shot, lob, and so forth. The position of your opponent should be a factor in playing the return shot. If he is in the center of the court and you have an easy return, play a passing shot, or use a lob shot to get him off the short line and put him farther back in the court. If your opponent is in the back court, or close to a side wall, a kill or placement shot may be used. As soon as you have returned the ball, get into position to play your opponent's return shot.

Keep your eye on the ball at all times. If your opponent is in back of you and you want to see the direction and speed of his return, look around but raise your arm so that your forearm will be in front of your face as a protection against being struck in the face by the returned ball. If your opponent is in front of you, watch the movement of his feet as he plays the ball. Frequently this permits you to detect the direction of the ball, which is quite an advantage.

If you have a good shot with your right hand at balls on the left side of the court, use it. If the ball is close to the left wall, use your left hand and don't force yourself out of position by trying to return the ball with your right hand. If you do, your opponent usually has a setup, or an easy return play.

BACK WALL PLAY

In your efforts for improvement, considerable attention should be given to your back wall play. As the player is usually facing the back wall when playing these back wall shots, they are difficult to make. They require more study, skill, control, and concentration than is required for most other shots.

Again, the way to learn is to start throwing the ball with sufficient speed so that it will strike first the front wall, the floor, and then the back wall. Catch it off the back wall. Then throw the ball so that it will strike first the front wall, then a side wall, the floor, and finally the back wall. This shot is used frequently in serving as well as in play. Watch the angle of these thrown balls as they come off the side and back walls. Anticipate ap-

Vic Hershkowitz making a high off the back wall shot. Beginners can learn much from this excellent action picture. Notice body position facing side wall—face toward back wall, eye on the ball, arm bent at the elbow, waiting for the ball to come to him. Body well balanced and in good position for his pivot and follow through when striking the ball. Carl Obert watches Vic and is poised ready to get in position to play Vic's return shot.

proximately where the ball should strike the back wall and take your position to catch it on the bounce.

Do not take your eyes off the ball in flight; do not chase it around the court; let it come to you, but take a position facing the back wall that will permit you to move quickly in or out to play it.

Another suggestion is to stand facing the back wall at a distance of about ten feet. Throw the ball to the back wall at varying heights and

Jimmy Jacobs playing a low off-the-back-wall shot. Ball first struck the floor, then the left side wall, then the back wall, and Jimmy is playing the ball on the fly as it comes off the back wall . . . an excellent action picture.

1

2

**Sequence C. Back and
Side Wall Corner Shots.**

5

Sequence C. Back and Side Wall Corner Shots. One of the most difficult plays for a beginner to attempt is playing a sharp angle ball that first strikes the floor, then strikes a side wall, and continues to the back wall requiring the receiver to play the ball on the fly as it comes off the back wall.

Sequence C gives an excellent and clear set of pictures showing the ball in flight and the techniques and skills required to properly play it. In (1) the ball has struck the left side wall and is on its way to the back wall. Oscar Obert stands facing the back and side walls. In (2) the ball is coming off the back wall and Oscar is getting set to play it. The position of his arm and body changes (3 and 4) as the ball approaches him and picture (5) shows the ball just being struck by the hand. (6) shows the ball on its way to the front wall with Oscar (7) facing the front wall completing his full body pivot.

These are excellent pictures and clearly show the splendid coordination of

3 4

6 7

body and arm in making this shot. You will notice in (5) that when the ball is struck Oscar's face is on a straight line with the ball. His stroke is so timed that when the hand meets the ball the hand is moving at its fastest speed giving the maximum power and drive to the ball.

Sequence C could also be used to illustrate the proper way to play a ball that first strikes the floor, the back wall, and then comes straight off the back wall on the fly. For example, the body position, arm motion, striking the ball, shifting of weight as the body pivots, and proper follow-through facing the front wall at the completion of the stroke are the same as shown in (3) to (7). A close examination of Sequence C clearly shows the proper position to take and the skills and techniques required to play these difficult back wall and corner shots. These pictures convey more clearly and graphically what a beginner should do and how he should do it than could be gained by reading a thousand words.

Oscar Obert showing proper position in playing a left-hand close-to-the-side wall shot. Ball has just come off the back wall after first striking the floor, side wall, and back wall—elbow slightly bent, hand cupped, feet well balanced, weight on right foot.

speeds. Study the rebound. Also, throw the ball first to the floor so that it will bounce to the back wall and then catch it on the fly. It will take concentration and timing to gauge correctly the speed and bounce of the balls off the back wall. Persistency and practice will pay off.

To play properly a ball coming off the right side of the back wall, assuming that you are a right-handed player, at least three-quarters of your body should be facing the back wall and left side wall. The eyes should face directly at the back wall, the feet are spread comfortably apart, and, as the ball comes to the player on the bounce or fly, the weight shifts to the right foot and the arm is raised to approximately shoulder height. With the elbow bent slightly and the hand cupped, the body starts to pivot and, when the player is facing the side wall, the ball is struck with a full follow-through motion. At the completion of the pivot and stroke, the player should be facing the front wall in a good position for the return play. Playing back wall shots depends on the angle, speed of the ball, and the distance the ball is from the back wall. Fundamentally, however, the procedure to follow in playing all back wall shots is to face the back wall and to keep your eye on the ball.

If you are a right-handed player, and you are playing a ball that has been hit hard at a sharp angle, and that has hit the floor, left side wall, and then the back wall, take your position facing the back wall and play the ball with your right hand as it comes off the wall, pivoting the body as you stroke the ball. If the angle of the ball in flight is such that, after it strikes the left side wall, it continues on to the back wall but remains close to the left side wall, not permitting a right-handed return, take your position facing the left side and back wall corner so as to return the ball with your left hand.

Whenever possible, without sacrificing position, play all balls off the back wall with your strong right hand. For left-handed players with a weak right hand the playing of these back wall shots should be reversed.

To handle back wall shots with any success at all demands a lot of practice. Ten or fifteen minutes with an experienced player showing how these shots should be played is very helpful.

CEILING SHOTS

The ceiling shot is used only when the ball is in play. If a served ball first hits the ceiling, the server's hand is out.

A good ceiling shot requires more control of the ball as to direction and speed than is required in almost any other shot. The ball is hit so as to strike first the ceiling close to the front wall and then the front wall. The rebound as it strikes the floor is high and the ball drops close to the back wall, in the corner if possible. In such cases, this is a very difficult ball to return with any degree of accuracy, as the player is forced to play the ball close to the back wall and usually near the floor.

The ceiling shot loses its effectiveness if the speed of the ball is such that it comes off the back wall, permitting a good back wall shot. It should be timed to drop lazily into the back corner without permitting any back or side wall play.

A ceiling ball is primarily used as a defensive shot, to get the opponent away from the front part of the court. An underhand stroke similar to an uppercut motion is usually used for the ceiling shot. For control and proper speed, the open hand slightly cupped gives the best results. Many experienced players use the fist ball in making ceiling shots, but this skill is acquired only after long practice.

Johnny Sloan says: "A well controlled ceiling shot is a strong asset particularly in forcing an opponent out of position, that is, usually away from

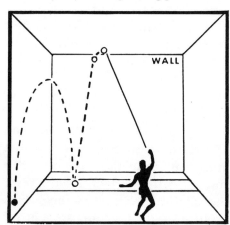

WALL

Ceiling shot.

the front court. When a player is off balance in playing the ball, or in the back court, the ceiling shot is a good defensive play as it permits the player to regain his position and get set for his opponent's return play. It is a difficult shot to master. It takes a lot of practice."

Carl Obert says: "Ceiling shots are really not for beginners, but when you are alone in the court try hitting the ceiling close to the front wall. It is a difficult shot. The ceiling shot is usually played when the ball is below the waist and the player is in the back court. By using an underhand upward motion, similar to an uppercut, the ball is struck so that it strikes the ceiling close to the front wall and, on its rebound from the floor, drops into one of the back wall corners. If properly controlled, these ceiling balls are hard to return with any degree of speed or accuracy."

KILL SHOTS

A good "kill" is one of the most effective shots in handball. It is beautiful to watch as the ball rolls out on the floor. The perfection of such a shot is the ambition of all. Considerable practice and concentration are required for a good kill shot. Its purpose is to have the ball come off the front wall as close to the floor as possible, so that it will just roll out on the floor or have a very low bounce, preventing a return play.

Do not attempt a kill shot unless you have an easy play—that is, a ball you can get set to play. Your body should be bent well over, facing the side wall, feet comfortably spread apart, and the ball struck when it is about ten to fifteen inches off the floor. At this height, the ball goes on to the front wall on a slightly descending line and, after hitting the front wall, rolls straight out or has little bounce. The higher off the floor the ball is hit, the sharper is the descending line to the front wall and consequently the higher the bounce as it comes off the front wall.

Johnny Sloan says: "Kill shots should be attempted only when you have an easy return shot, a shot you can get set for. Keep your eye on the ball and strike it when it is about a foot or so off the floor. Aim (in four wall) to hit in the corner of the front and side walls depending on the position of your opponents. It is rather difficult to kill a ball which is struck when it is three or four feet off the floor. As a rule, such a ball has a tendency, after it strikes the front wall, to bounce high enough to permit a return play. Keep your kill shot returns low."

Keep your attempted kill shots as low as possible. Attempting a kill on high bouncing balls with an overhand stroke is not good. It seldom works out.

Another suggestion for kill shots is to take advantage of the side and front walls—that is, the corner shots. Direct the ball so that it will first strike the side wall close to the floor and then strike the front wall. In many cases, the ball just rolls out. Or aim the ball so as to strike the front wall close to the floor and then strike the side wall. Either of these shots reduces the bounce of the ball as compared to the ball coming straight off

A good action picture of Oscar Obert, who has just hit the ball to the right corner for a kill shot. Study this picture for proper body balance, knee position, concentration, and follow-through motion of the arm.

the front wall. In many cases, in playing lower corner kills, the ball will strike the side and front wall simultaneously, thus preventing any play of the ball at all.

Vic Hershkowitz says: "Killing fly balls is more difficult than killing balls which bounce off the floor. More control and accuracy is necessary. A fly kill should only be attempted if the player is in the front part of the court, in good position, and his opponent is off balance or in the back court. However, this shot should be added to your repertoire and practiced frequently."

Summing up the suggestions on "kill" shots it is the consensus of opinion among the top-flight players that the most effective kill shot is the ball that first strikes low on a side wall, close to the front wall, and then strikes the front wall. This low hit ball comes off the side wall at a sharp angle hitting the front wall, which reduces its bounce off the floor and, with its sharp angle and very low (if any) bounce, makes it very difficult to return.

A low returned ball that first strikes the front wall and then the side wall has a tendency to bounce higher off the floor, affording a better opportunity to play the ball than the ball that hits first a side wall and then the front wall at a sharp angle.

Oscar Obert, who possesses one of the best kill shots, says, "A low kill shot ball which first strikes the side wall and then hits the front wall on an angle is 'going away' from the opponent while the low kill shot which first hits the front wall and then the side wall is 'coming at you' and as a result is easier to return."

Many attempted kill shots where the ball first hits the front wall—say about six inches or so off the floor—and then comes straight back (without striking a side wall) will permit a return play by an alert opponent. If this same ball, however, had first hit the side wall about six inches off the floor and then hit the front wall, the bounce off the floor would be greatly reduced and with the sharp angle would make it very difficult to return.

Practice the two-wall kill shot.

DOUBLES

Doubles is a very popular game. While most of the young players prefer a singles game, which requires more speed and energy, still, a good doubles game, with young or old players of about equal ability, is exciting and enjoyable.

Two good players do not necessarily make a good doubles team. Before starting the game, an understanding between partners as to who will play the front court and who the back court is advisable. If both partners are right-handed players, the one with the better left hand should play the left side.

When the game starts, watch the play of your opponents to establish their weaknesses and court covering and play to these weaknesses. Your opponents are going to play to your weakness, too, so prepare some defense for it.

In four-wall doubles, the server may start serving from any part of the service zone. His partner must stand within the service box with his back to the wall until the ball passes the short line on each serve. If the server's partner is hit by a served fly ball while he is standing in the service box, it counts as a dead ball but does not eliminate any shorts or faults preceding the serve. If a partner, while standing in the service box, is hit by a served ball on the bounce, it is a short ball. If a good served ball strikes the partner while the latter is outside the service box, the hand is out. In championships and tournaments you can direct your serves continuously to any one of your opponents. It is not necessary to alternate serves, that is, to serve first to one opponent and then to the other. However, in club doubles, pickup games, the alternate service should be the rule. It makes for a more even and satisfying game.

More complete rules for doubles are listed in the synopsis of four-wall rules on page 77.

Johnny Sloan and Phil Collins, probably one of the best teams in handball history, play with Collins up front taking all the low balls and Sloan in the back court taking all back court and ceiling shots.

Phil Collins says: "Good team play and planned strategy are essential. Before starting the game plan your offensive and defensive play. Determine which one should play the left and which the right side. Decide on the strategy to be followed in playing front court, back court and particularly in four wall, the angle shots. While the ball is in play, will each partner play all balls, front or back court, which are in his territory? Or, should one player play all front court low balls and his partner all long backcourt balls? To avoid confusion and getting in each others way, this strategy should be decided upon before starting to play. A player should not, as they say, "hog the court." By doing so, the player forces himself out of position and completely upsets his partner."

In doubles, court position is important. If both partners are up front, it is not advisable for the opponents to attempt a kill, or a low passing shot, as either one would have to be perfect. A better return would be a high fast ball around the walls, or a lob, so as to get your opponents away from the short line. Another suggestion, in a case like this, is to try a fast return ball about waist high down the center of the court. Both partners may attempt to play this center court ball and be off balance, make a weak return, or miss it completely.

Another good court position is for a player to be up front and his partner in the back court. The latter directs most of his returns in the direction of his partner, thus requiring the opponents to go around the partner in order to play the ball. In plays like this, care should be taken no hinder is committed.

Ruby Obert says: "In one-wall particularly, partners should plan their strategy and follow it as closely as possible. There are no back or side walls to help you, so playing position is very important. If a player consistently plays balls which could be better played by his partner, he leaves himself out of position. His opponents will take advantage of this and play a fast angle shot which will have to be chased and returned by the player who may be outside the playing area of the court."

HINDERS

The hinder rule is the most controversial one in handball. For some reason or other the hinder rule for four-wall is quite different from the one-wall rule. In four-wall the rule clearly states that "A player who unintentionally interferes with an opponent in such a way as to prevent him from having a fair chance to return the ball" commits a hinder. The rule further states: "It is the duty of the side that has played the ball to get out of the way of their opponents." This hinder rule is quite clear and every effort should be made to comply with it.

In refereed games, it is the duty of the referee to call all hinders, but beginners, in their pickup games and in learning to play, will not have a referee and these hinders will have to be decided among themselves.

A ball in play that strikes an opponent before striking the floor is a

Illustrating a "hinder" play. Carl Obert (front) is prevented from properly swinging at the ball as Vic Hershkowitz is standing too close to him.

hinder. This is true even if a ball ricochets off a player's hand backward, sideward, or downward, and hits an opponent before it hits the floor, even though it has no chance of reaching the front wall. It is a hinder.

Give your opponent a FAIR chance to play the ball; do not cross in front of your opponent as he is about to play the ball; do not crowd, back up, or stand close to your opponent to the extent that you may interfere with his return shot.

In doubles, when a player is interfered with by his partner, it is not a hinder.

A straddled ball—that is, a ball passing between the legs of the player or side having just played it—is not necessarily a hinder. If, however, a ball passes between the legs of the player who has just played the ball and the receiver does not have a fair chance to play it, it is a hinder.

In the rules, there is a section on "Avoidable Hinders" that, if committed, will result in a point or handout, as the case may be. Generally speaking, these are deliberate acts on the part of the player to interfere with his opponent's attempt to play the ball. These acts are unsportsmanlike and should not be committed.

It is suggested that beginners read and study Section 5 of the Unified Rules on hinders, and follow the rules. This makes for a better understanding and helps to eliminate disputes and misunderstandings.

We all want to win our games; there is no question about that. Every fair effort should be directed to that end. However, a full compliance with the hinder rule, giving your opponent a fair chance to play the ball, will assure a very friendly and enjoyable game.

COURT STRATEGY

As a beginner, all of your efforts should be concentrated on improving your control of the ball—that is, in speed and direction—stepping up the speed as you improve. However, a few hints on court strategy might be helpful.

The old cliche "Hit it where they ain't" applies to handball as well as to other sports. All balls should be played so as not to give your adversary a setup; keep him out of position, off balance. This requires quick thinking and, as your opponent is thinking the same way, it boils down to a battle of wits, outguessing each other. With players about equal in ability, a most interesting and pleasant game results.

1. Assume player A is in the front center court and B, playing the ball, is in the back court and has a good shot at the ball. It would not be advisable for B to attempt a kill shot for it would have to be perfect since A, in the front court, could conceivably play the ball if it came off the front wall with just a slight bounce and probably kill it. In this instance, B should attempt a ceiling or passing shot, or a hard hit ball around the walls to force A out of position and away from the front court.

2. Assume A is in the front court but close to the left side wall; B, playing the ball, is in the center of the court near the right wall. A expects B to take advantage of the open right side and play the ball in that direction. As B gets set to play the ball, A, anticipating that B will attempt to play it there, moves in the direction of the open court. B, expecting A's action, should play the ball in such a way that it comes off the front wall to A's left, the left side of the court. This play usually finds A out of position and results in a miss or a weak return.

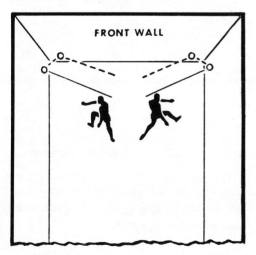

Corner shots.

3. A and B are both up front near the short line, A on the left side, B on the right. B is playing the ball and a good return shot would be to strike the left side wall about three or four feet high, then hit the front wall and bounce at a sharp angle to the right of the court as illustrated on page 53. This forces A to react very fast to play the ball and gives him a difficult shot, resulting in a weak return or miss.

In serving and while the ball is in play, take advantage of the side walls as much as possible. A ball coming off the front wall so directed as to strike a side wall could hit at the junction of the floor and the wall, causing the ball to skid, take an unexpected bounce, and come off the side wall at a sharp angle, or the ball could hug the wall. All these possibilities could result in misses or weak returns by your opponent. The law of averages will give you many of these "breaks."

There are two very effective passing shots: one, when the ball is played low and fast up and down the court, not striking a side or back wall; the second, when a hard hit ball first strikes the front wall about five feet high, then a side wall, passing the receiver on the fly, and continuing to the opposite side wall corner, preventing a good return play.

Both of these passing shots should not be played with so much speed that a return could be made off the side or back wall. The decision to play the first rather than the second depends on the position of both players.

An excellent action shot of young Buzz Schumate, Denver YMCA, getting set to play a side wall shot, ball coming off the side wall. Eye on the ball, arm bent at elbow, body well balanced. Dick Langdon, Minneapolis YMCA, getting set for Buzz's return play. Photo by Martin Schneider through the courtesy of the USHA.

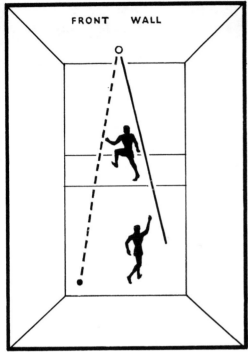

FRONT   WALL

Passing shot.

The player to be passed should be up front; the player hitting the ball should be in back with a good opportunity to control the shot as to direction and speed.

Another situation is that in which both players are up front, A at the short line and B a few feet in front of him. B has hit the ball and A has a good return shot. A's return shot should be a hard hit passing shot or a soft "lob." Care should be taken, however, to see that the speed of the ball does not carry to the back wall, giving B an easy return. In this case, B being close to the front wall, A could return the ball hard and low so that it will strike the floor at the feet of B, catching him off balance and out of position. This usually results in a very weak return or miss.

All these plays come with practice, and with watching more experienced players. Try these shots earnestly and profit by the trial and error system.

If the ball in play is close to a side wall or as they say is "hugging" the wall, do not take a full hard swing. Your hand is apt to hit the side wall causing a serious injury. In playing these close to the wall shots, play it safe, use a slow pushing or sweep stroke—just try to get the ball back to the front wall.

The following *advice from Al Stein* should be read carefully. Al Stein for over 30 years has been the Athletic Director of the 92d Street YMHA in New York City with approximately 4,500 members. He has a wealth of experience in athletically developing young men, particularly in handball.

"As a rule you will find a chart of hints and advice for beginners posted on the bulletin board wherever handball is played to any extent. Beginners should read and be familiar with these hints, tips and pointers and try them out on the court while practicing or in play without any concern with winning.

"Watch good players in action, observe their techniques in serving, footwork, strokes, and shot making. Ask questions on the plays you don't quite understand and profit by concentration on what you have seen and heard. The most basic play for the beginner is to hit the ball, either hand, with the same flexible forearm and wrist snap motion. Combining the forearm and wrist motion with direction and control plus attention to footwork will give the novice the essential equipment toward rapid development as a handball player.

"Playing occasionally with a more experienced player or an instructor who will offer suggestions to correct your apparent weaknesses will soon show results.

"Dedicated purposeful practice will make the beginner a handball player and the handball player a winner.

"One final and very important word. Get into condition and stay in shape."

IMMORTALS OF FOUR-WALL HANDBALL

In the history of four-wall handball two names, Joe Platak and Al Banuet, will be recorded as probably the Babe Ruth and Ty Cobb of handball. The author had the good fortune of knowing Banuet and Platak very well and watched them play many times.

Al Banuet.

Joe Platak.

Colorful Al Banuet, of the Olympic Club San Francisco, in his early twenties electrified handball fans throughout the country with his devastating fist shots using left or right hand with equal skill. His control and speed of the ball even when playing back wall shots with his fists have been unequaled. He was the best exponent of the fist ball ever to appear on a handball court. He easily swept through three National AAU Four-Wall Championships in 1929, 1930, 1931 and then while still in his early twenties terminated his amateur status by turning to professional boxing as a career.

Joe Platak (now deceased) of the Lake Shore Athletic Club, Chicago, Ill., was a real perfectionist. No player was ever in better physical condition than Joe when he stepped into the court for a championship tournament. He trained diligently for all championships, doing miles of road work and rope skipping and hours of practicing. He was completely ambidextrous, killing effectively with either hand, and seemed tireless in going through a hard tournament. He won nine National AAU Four Wall titles in singles, seven in a row 1935 to 1941 inclusive, repeating again in 1943 and 1945. During the 7 years of national championship play he did not lose a single game.

What success our later champions Jimmy Jacobs, Johnny Sloan, and Oscar Obert would have against Banuet and Platak is hard to say as these young fellows are still making championship records. However, I feel sure that any one of them pitted against either of these two immortals would have given an excellent account of himself.

4

One-Wall Handball

AMERICAN ORIGIN

One-wall handball is strictly an American game, and its activities are confined chiefly to the Metropolitan New York City area, although there are a few one-wall courts in cities like Philadelphia and Miami Beach. One-wall handball is played in New York's parks, playgrounds, recreation centers, and beach resorts. It is played outdoors all year around by thousands of young and middle-aged men who find it an excellent and enjoyable form of exercise. Dry footing is all that is needed regardless of how cold it may be. Snowfall of 23 inches has been cleared in order to play outdoor one-wall handball. For those interested in physical fitness, exercise, and relaxation, outdoor one-wall handball is highly recommended.

One-wall handball is probably the most popular of all the athletic and recreational games available in parks and playgrounds in New York City. A Novice Tournament sponsored by a New York City newspaper attracts each year approximately 1,700 boys, 800 girls and 3,300 men (between 5,500 and 6,000 entries). There are about 1,850 one-wall courts in the New York City parks and playgrounds, with hundreds more at beach resorts, swimming pools, and schools. As many as 1,500 spectators in a specially built stadium can be accommodated for matches at the Brighton Beach Baths. On the indoor courts at the Brownsville Boys Club in Brooklyn as many as 1,000 spectators are on hand for championship events.

STANDARD SIZE COURT

Standard specifications of a one-wall court are:

Wall. The wall shall be 20 feet in width from the outside edge of each sideline and 16 feet high.

Floor. The floor shall be 20 feet in width between the outside edges of the sidelines. It shall be 34 feet from the wall to the back edge of the long line. The sidelines should be extended at least three feet further from

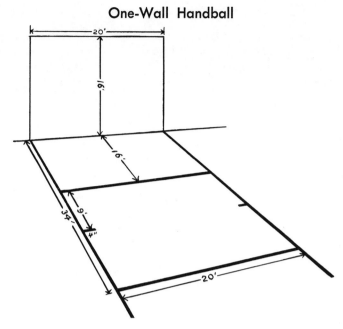

Dimensions of a standard one-wall court.

the wall than the long line. There should be a minimum of six feet of floor outside each sideline and in back of long line to allow sufficient movement area for players.

Short Line. This runs parallel with the front wall between the sidelines with its back edge 16 feet from the wall.

Service Markers. There shall be service markers (lines) at least six inches long parallel to and midway between the short and long lines, extending inward from the sidelines. The imaginary further extension and joining of these markings indicate the *Service Line*.

Service Zone. This is the floor area inside and including the short, side-, and service lines (or markers).

Receiving Zone. This is the floor area in back of the short line, bounded by and including the long and sidelines in which area all legally served balls must strike the floor, except when the served ball is played on the fly by the receiver.

Playing Zone. After the ball is legally served, the playing zone is the floor area between the front wall and the long line, and between the sidelines and including these lines.

POSITION OF PLAYERS

Serving Side. Server must start and complete his service within the serving zone.

Receiver must stand back of the service lines (or markers) until the served ball passes the short line.

Doubles. Server must start and complete his service within the serving zone. His partner must stand outside the sideline astraddle the service markers and cannot enter the receiving zone until the served ball passes him.

The receiving side must stand in back of the service markers until the served ball passes the short line. It is not required that the receiving side stand in the receiving zone while the ball is being served. The side may stand in back of the long line or outside of the sidelines if it wants to.

With few exceptions, such as service, hinders, side, and long line penalties, the Unified Handball Rules apply to both one- and four-wall. As a beginner you should read the Unified One-Wall Handball Rules. This knowledge will help you enjoy the game and will eliminate arguments and misunderstandings.

Familiarize yourself with the fundamentals that apply to all handball games (one-, three-, and four-wall), such as "Getting the Feel of the Ball," "Hitting the Ball," "Stance," "Playing the Ball," "Handball Strokes," and so forth.

CONTROL

In one-wall handball, control is probably the most important factor. A player should practice hitting angle, crosscourt, and fly balls, *concentrating on keeping the ball within the side and long lines.* The next in importance to control is to develop a fast ball. Control and a fast ball are essential for any advancement in one-wall ratings.

One-wall handball requires many quick starts, steps, and speed in getting into position to play the ball. Playing sharply angled balls may require a player to be as far as three feet outside of the sideline to return the ball;

Typical one-wall court in the parks and playgrounds in New York City.

his next move is then to get back on the court in position to play his opponent's return shot. This takes fast footwork.

In one-wall handball, you have to "go and get the ball." In four-wall, because of the assistance of the side and back wall, you can "let the ball come to you." In one-wall, once the ball passes you, it's gone! Therefore, you have to move fast to be in a position to return the ball. A good part of your practice periods should be spent in returning balls off the wall with either right or left hand, particularly those angle balls that take you outside the court to make a return. These angle shots are very difficult to handle and require a great deal of practice.

WEAK HAND

If you are a right-handed player, a lot of your practice should be spent on strengthening your weak hand. In order not to be repetitious, we ask you to read pages 23 to 25 on the weak hand. In one-wall more effort should be made in developing your weak hand than in four-wall. Defensive control and accuracy are far more important than in four-wall, as there are no side or back walls to assist you. In many cases, you may be even from one to five feet outside the court when playing the ball. You should not sacrifice court position by returning left side court balls with your right hand. Probably the most difficult play in one-wall handball is to return sharply angled, high bouncing balls with your weak hand, particularly while standing outside the court. The average player uses a straight-arm sweeping motion in returning these angle shots since it gives more control over the ball than when he uses the regular "bent at the elbow" overhand stroke. Practice with the weak hand is our strong recommendation—develop it.

Ruby Obert says: "In tournament games you are as strong as your weak hand. Your opponents will direct most of their shots to your weak hand, which is quite a handicap for you to handle.

"As a beginner, in addition to practicing with your weak hand, try serving with it whenever you can find a player inferior to you. Do not try to win the game as much as to develop yourself. In the long run you will have profited more by this than if you had won the game by using your strong hand continuously."

Vic Hershkowitz says: "A weak hand is a target for your oppenents. So, while developing your strong arm by no means overlook your weak arm. Do not force yourself out of position to return a ball with your strong arm when you should have used your weak arm. This does not mean to do so if you have a 'cripple'—use the 'money' hand. My advice is simple. Play the ball with your weak hand on the bounce off the front wall, keeping it in play as long as you can. Then try returning the ball on the fly using both hands. The position of your feet and proper body balance should be carefully studied to get best timing and leverage."

Here you have, for the development of your weak hand, suggestions from two of the best players in the country.

SIDE ARM, OVERHAND STROKES

The side arm stroke is used rather exclusively in one-wall. It is made faster, propels the ball with greater speed and can be delivered at a sharper angle than by using the underhand stroke.

However, the underhand stroke should not be entirely neglected, as it should be used when playing very low bouncing balls coming off the wall. Many players find the underhand stroke very effective when serving the "hook" ball.

In one-wall handball, a good overhand stroke is important, as it is used both offensively and defensively. When the volley consists of overhand back court play, the players try to maneuver each other out of position in order to set up an easy return play, a kill or passing shot. Usually the overhand stroke results in a high bounding return ball, which should be played on the upward bounce. This requires proper timing and control. With a wall only 16 feet high, and no ceiling or side walls to help, any return from the deep court must be well directed and controlled so as not to give your adversary an easy play, such as a waist line or short line fly ball.

HOW TO SERVE

The most powerful and effective weapon in one-wall handball is the service. There are more "aces" scored in one-wall than in four-wall because there are no side or back walls to help the receiver and the short line is only 16 feet from the wall. Accuracy, speed, and deception on serves should be given a great deal of attention.

However, as a beginner your problem is one of control and direction— speed comes later. Your purpose is to serve the ball so that it will elude or at least give your opponent a rather difficult shot to return. As a rule, particularly in tournaments, you direct most of your serves to your opponent's weakness. This requires control, proper stance, good balance, easy pivot as you stroke the ball, your follow-through, depending on the type of serve you are going to make.

Because of the large serving area many players take a step or two forward before striking the ball when serving low power balls. This is for added momentum, giving more power in hitting the ball. This type of serve is for the more experienced player. You are chiefly concerned with control and direction. Keep your opponent guessing, off balance if possible.

Vic Hershkowitz says: "Try to develop at least one good serve. Service is about 60% of a game. There are four or five effective serves, such as the lob, cross court, fast ball, and sharp angle. Try them out. Mix them up until you find the one best suited to your style. Make this your 'Sunday' serve but keep mixing them up."

TYPES OF SERVICE

Most of the top-flight players have a variety of serves to meet varied conditions. The serve quite often is the low, hard hit shot that is directed to hit the floor just over the short line and close to the sideline to force the receiver to return it while on the run or off balance. The direction of this low, hard-hit serve depends on the position of the receiver and on the strength of his weak hand. If, for example, you want to deliver a hard-hit low-angle ball to strike the floor just over the short line and close to the right sideline, the server might stand in the serving area near the left line, to get as much angle as possible. This angled serve forces the receiver to return the ball while his arm or foot may be outside the sideline as illustrated by "B" below.

Many players stand in the center of the serving area and serve low hard-hit balls to either the right or left sidelines, depending upon the position of the receiver and his weakness. This center position gives the server a good position for playing the return shot.

Another effective serve is the high soft lob that, after striking high on the wall, hits the floor and takes a high bounce. This serve usually forces the receiver to play the ball on the up bounce, resulting in a defensive shot and many times an easy return play by the server. In playing some of these soft lob balls a receiver may step forward and play the ball on the fly thus catching the server out of position. The server should always keep his eye on the ball in flight and be ready for any ball returned on the fly. Note that, by the rules, a receiver cannot step in over the service line to play a served ball. For a straight out high lob serve, the same stroke and bounce of the ball applies as shown in the illustration on page 40.

The overhand serve requires a lot of control and is very effective when served properly. Server stands in the service area, say close to the right

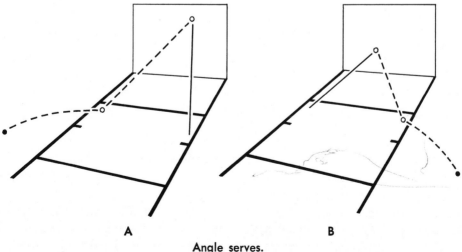

A   B

Angle serves.

sideline, and serves the ball with a hard overhand stroke so that the ball will strike the wall and then rebound to the floor over the short line and near the left sideline (as illustrated above in "B"). It then takes a high bounce and the receiver is forced out of the court to play it. It is a difficult shot to make as the receiver must return the ball so that it hits the front wall and then strikes the floor within the playing area. He must also get back into the court quickly for the server's play of the ball. This requires good control and fast footwork for the receiver. This hard-hit overhand serve is also effective when the server sees the receiver standing in the back court closer to the left sideline. He then plays the serve straight down the right sideline near the long line, catching the receiver out of position for a good return.

In one-wall particularly, a well-controlled hook serve to the right or left is the strong offensive serve. In addition to scoring many aces, its purpose is to force the receiver to play the ball while off balance, or out of position, resulting in a weak return. The most effective hop serves are the ones that strike the floor close to the long line, or at the feet of the receiver, seldom affording the receiver a good return shot. This hook serve should be attempted only when a player has improved to the extent that he has confidence in his control, speed, and placements. How to execute the hook or hop serve is covered on pages 26 to 28 and page 41.

A player who has good control of a variety of serves and uses them properly has a decided advantage over a player who consistently uses a "pet" serve. The server tries to keep the receiver guessing. A good baseball pitcher with an assortment of pitches keeps the batter guessing so that he cannot get set for any pitch. If the pitcher used only a fast ball, the batter would know what to expect and would get set for it. The same is true in handball: A low hard-hit ball on every serve would permit the receiver to get set for it, expect it. So mix them up.

RECEIVER

The receiver must stand back of the service line until the served ball passes the short line. He usually stands in the center of the court close to the long line. If the receiver's left hand is weak, he will usually stand a foot or so nearer the left sideline. His body should be bent over a little, somewhat like an infielder in baseball—feet spread apart, weight on the soles of the feet, eye on the ball, ready to move as soon as the ball is served.

As the ball is served, the decision as to how it will be returned, whether by a kill, a passing shot, or simply a defensive shot, depends on the speed and direction of the served ball, the position of the server, and whether or not you have a good shot at the ball.

In returning a hook serve, do not try to take it on the rise from the floor, since the ball starts its hooked path when it strikes the floor and you are apt to miss it completely or it may glance off your hand. If the hook ball bounces—say two to three feet in front of you—let the ball take its hook

Good action picture. Ruby Obert serving. Carl Obert receiving. Beginners should study body position of each player. Ruby with eye on ball, arm bent at elbow, hand cupped. Carl well poised, ready to go to the left or right as soon as ball is hit.

and be ready to go quickly to your right or left to play it. If the ball strikes the floor close to your feet, you must try to hit it before the hook can take effect. This means that you try to "scoop" it immediately as it comes off the floor. These are difficult balls to return with any degree of speed or direction. Just try a defensive shot to return the ball to the front wall.

On the hard-hit overhand sharp-angle serves that may require you to go outside the court to return them, concentrate on returning the ball high on the wall, so as to give you an opportunity to get back on the court before the server can get set for his play.

Carl Obert says: "Beginners should practice using the 'scoop' stroke. In one-wall particularly a cardinal rule is 'don't let the ball get passed you' for you haven't got a side or back wall to help you. Consequently, while the ball is in play, many hard hit balls will hit the floor at the feet of the receiver necessitating a fast 'scooping' motion of the hand to play the ball as it immediately starts to rise from the floor. You can't get set for these shots or play them on the fly and the only way to return them is with a 'scooping' motion. Practice this shot as you will be called on frequently to use it."

"FLY" BALL, PUNCH BALL

A "fly" ball is one that you strike before it hits the floor. If you watch top-flight one-wall players in action, you will quickly see the importance of being proficient in playing fly balls. In one-wall, you should not let the ball get past you. In many cases, this requires returning the ball on the fly. Since a ball can come at you very fast, often your only play is to return it on the fly. Hitting on the fly is also a good offensive shot, since you frequently catch your opponent off guard or out of position. A good position for playing fly balls is in the center of the court close to the short line. You are then in an excellent position for playing a passing, an angle, or a kill shot with either hand. Your opponent is at a disadvantage, no matter which it is.

Vic Hershkowitz is probably the most skillful player of fly balls on the courts today. He has scored many points and won many games by his well-directed fly ball placements, kills, and passing shots. His advice to beginners is to spend a lot of practice time in playing fly balls.

The "punch" ball is not used by many one-wall players, particularly beginners. Unless one has excellent control of the shot, it should not be used. It is hard to handle. It is a defensive shot, used quite frequently in four-wall, where control is not as necessary as in one-wall. It is not advisable for a beginner in one-wall to attempt a punch-ball shot. Information on the punch ball is given on page 29.

KILL SHOTS

A good kill shot is the ambition of every handball player. Beginners should practice making this shot, since nothing in handball is more rewarding and no play gives more pleasure than to see your shot strike low on the front wall and roll out on the floor. In one-wall particularly, accuracy is very important when playing kill shots to either side edge. The ball coming off the wall must hit the floor in fair territory and not outside the court, which happens on many angled kill shots. Unfortunately, many players attempt to kill almost every ball they hit, even if they are in back court, or off balance. A kill shot should be attempted only when the player is in a good position and can get set for the shot; the position of his opponent should also be a factor.

The kill shot is attempted more frequently in one-wall than in four-wall. In one-wall an angled kill shot that strikes the wall low, then the floor, and continues at a sharp angle is a very difficult ball to play. In playing these low angle killed shots, it is not uncommon to see an opponent fall flat on the floor in his efforts to return the ball.

For proper position, stance, and stroke when making the kill shot, see pages 48 to 50.

Oscar Obert has about the best "kill" shot for one- or four-walls. Here is what he has to say: "Consistently hitting the lower part of the front wall is very difficult and comes only after long practice. A "kill" shot can be played on the bounce or on the fly, but always remember in attempting a kill shot to bend your body as low as possible with more flexing at the knees."

HINDERS

The hinder rule in one-wall is very simple but, for some reason or other, it causes a great deal of discussion. The rule says, in substance, that if a player in front, after having hit the ball, stands perfectly still, does not sway, bend, or move in any way, the receiver is required to play the ball even though he may not be in a position to see it. The ball may even have bounced at the feet or close to the side of the player who hit it. Some say that the rule is unfair or unsportsmanlike, and that the receiver must have a fair chance to return the ball. Others defend the rule by saying that a player exhibits skill and control to cause a ball to hit the floor close to him and it is up to the receiver to find some way to play it.

If the player in front who just hit the ball moves to a new position in front of the receiver or moves backward, interfering with the receiver, it is a hinder ball.

If the receiver is in front of his opponent and, in moving back to play the ball, contacts his opponent, it is a hinder.

A ball in play that strikes an opponent before striking the wall or floor, even though the opponent may be standing outside the court, or in back, is a hinder and must be played over. For a more detailed account of hinders and avoidable hinders, see the section on Hinders, pages 51 to 53.

COURT STRATEGY

As a beginner, your efforts should be centered on direction and speed of the ball. Until these are developed to the point that you have some control over them, no difficult shots or position play should be attempted. Please read the first two paragraphs on Court Strategy on page 53. However, by watching experienced one-wall players you can quickly see the importance of good court strategy.

The position of yourself and your opponent is one of the essential factors of court strategy. A good position in the center of the court near the short line is very desirable. You are, then, in a position to try a kill, a passing, or an angle shot, keeping your opponent off balance and out of position. Never give your opponent a setup if you can help it. If he is on the right or left side of the court, force him to the opposite side to play your return. If your opponent returns the ball from the back court, your best move is to try to play the ball on the fly, going for a kill or a sharp angle shot.

If your opponent is on your left, your return ball should be directed to hit the floor on your right close to where you are standing. If you stand perfectly still, you are not committing a hinder and your opponent will have a difficult shot at the ball.

When your opponent is up front and you have a good clear shot, attempt a passing shot. If your opponent has taken a good position near the short line center and you are in the back court, your returns should be directed to force him away from the center of the court. In such a case it is not advisable for you, being in the back court, to attempt a kill shot. It would have to be perfect; the percentage is against you. Depending on how far back you are, try a waist-high passing shot or perhaps, if the ball is high enough, try a hard-hit overhand stroke.

Whenever there is an equal chance of hitting right or left, hit to the side of your opponent's weaker hand.

Mickey Blechman, Chairman of the Metropolitan AAU Handball Committee and an authority on one-wall handball, has this advice for beginners: "After years of playing and watching the steady improvement of many young men in one-wall handball I can say that there is no panacea for success. There is no substitute for constant practice.

"Remember you are a beginner—don't expect to become a champ quickly or to imitate one. Here are some basic considerations for you to follow:

"Get your body in proper position before you hit the ball.

Know where you want to hit the ball before you hit it.

Keep your hand slightly cupped when hitting the ball.

Practice hitting the ball on the fly.

Don't try to overpower the ball. Speed will increase naturally as you practice and gain experience.

Ask some good player to show you proper body and feet position, arm motion, pivot, follow-through.

When possible use the side arm swing in playing the ball.

On all low bouncing balls strike the ball on its descent, not on the rise.

On all high bouncing balls if possible strike it on the rise, follow-through motion rather than chopping at the ball.

Hit underhand only as a last resort. There is less power than when using the side arm swing.

In practice aim for a spot on the wall, not a "bounce spot" on the floor.

Practice defensive play. See how many times you can return the ball to the front wall before missing—using both hands.

Give your "off hand" a lot of practice—develop it—very important.

Whenever you have a possible choice hit the ball with your natural hand. All things being equal, the stronger return comes from the natural or good hand. There has never been a player whose two hands were really of equal strength.

If you play outdoors always wear enough clothing to keep you warm.

Don't play with an injury. You may increase the severity of the injury and you may subconsciously favor the injury and throw your normal game off.

When you see that your game is off, ease up. No one is great at all times. Swing slowly, regain timing, go only for safe shots, your game will come back."

5

Tournaments

DUTIES OF A REFEREE

The success of tournaments and championships depends to a great extent on the referee. His experience, knowledge of the rules, control of the game, and quick, firm decisions are important factors in successful tournaments. Capable and experienced referees should be available for all championships.

The referee is the sole arbiter of all plays and his decisions are final. The rules state: "The Referee shall decide all questions which may arise during the game. His decision shall be in accordance with these rules. He shall be the sole judge of all illegally served balls, as defined in these rules: hinders, avoidable hinders, unfair tactics, stalling, or unnecessarily delaying play. His decisions are final. He has the authority to forfeit a match. Any player refusing to abide by the decision of the Referee forfeits the match."

Before starting a four-wall match the referee should have the assistance of a scorekeeper and have on hand an extra handball or two, a copy of the rule book, score sheet, pencils, and towels. In addition to the above essentials a referee for all one-wall matches should have three linesmen, one for each sideline and one for the long line.

The referee should ask the players if there are any rules they wish to have clarified, or any questions they would like to ask. He should explain any house or court rules to be observed.

The referee should introduce the players to each other, if they have not already met, and then introduce the players to the spectators, giving name, club represented, handball titles held.

The toss of the coin determines who will serve first. A ball acceptable to both players should be used. Referee says, "Play ball," and the game is on.

The referee should make immediate call on all foot faults, hinders, longs, shorts, balls that are hit on the second bounce. He should not hesitate or wait until the end of the volley, or until an appeal by a player. Immediate calls eliminate discussions and delays.

The referee should request the cooperation of the spectators by asking them to refrain from rooting, or making remarks while the ball is in play. When the play is over, then applause is permissible.

He should keep the spectators and players informed of the progress of the game. Before each player starts to serve, the score should be announced —for example, 16 playing 14. After each point is scored, the total should be announced.

If a player should question the ruling of the referee, his reasoning should be carefully considered. The referee should explain his decision or ruling. If the referee then believes that he has made an error, he should change his decision. The changing of a decision by the referee is an admission of human error and does not reflect on the ability of the referee.

A referee should not be influenced by any remarks from spectators or players. He is the sole judge of all plays.

If the referee suspects a player of unnecessarily crowding, pushing, not giving his opponent a legal shot at the ball, he should issue a warning. If the player persists in his unfair tactics, the referee should apply the penalty under the rules.

The referee should remind the players that they cannot leave the court without his permission. Between the first and second games a two-minute rest period is allowed. A ten-minute rest period is allowed between the second and third games. Players must be ready to resume playing at the end of each of these periods.

The referee should not permit players to call shorts, hinders, good or bad balls, ball hit his opponent, etc. However, there are instances on very close plays where a player can be of assistance to the referee. On a questionable play, say a low ball, a player may say "I missed it," "two bounces," or "the ball hit me." The ball may have brushed the player and not be noticed by the referee. However, on such plays, the player should immediately make his call and not wait for the rebound of the ball from the front wall. The referee may or may not accept the call of the player on these questionable plays. The decision is the referee's alone.

Any player continually questioning the decision of the referee, engaging in unsportsmanlike tactics, delaying the game, stamping his feet, slapping the wall, etc., should be warned by the referee to desist on penalty of a forfeit. If he persists, the game should be forfeited.

While a ball is in play, a player is not permitted to stop or catch the ball and say: "The ball is wet," or "The ball is broken." If he does, it is a point or handout, as the case may be. He should play the ball and, when the volley is over, call the attention of the referee to the alleged wet or broken ball.

The referee should see that the server is not serving a "wet" ball. He should occasionally check the gloves if they appear to be wet. During a long volley the ball may come in contact with sweaty clothes or gloves. If there is any doubt in his mind, the referee should examine the ball and wipe any wet spots dry.

Refereeing a doubles match requires exceptional alertness and is a very tough job. Four men on court, quick moves, and jockeying for position frequently result in body contact and hinders. The referee's calls should be made very speedily in doubles.

SCORE SHEETS

For minor tournaments, pickup matches where a detailed account of the game as to kills, errors, passing and ceiling shots, and aces made during the game is not too important, there are a number of score sheets in use that simply record the points as scored. The most popular score sheet is the one with twenty-one boxes (as illustrated), one box for each point as scored. The open check above and below the box indicates the player serving and the line drawn through the check indicates the hand out.

SCORE SHEET FOR STATISTICS OF THE GAME

For those who are interested in the statistics of the game and in order to evaluate a player's strength and weakness by keeping a record of aces, kills, errors passing, and ceiling shots, an official score sheet was approved by the Unified Rules Committee.[1] This detailed account is interesting as

Score sheet.

[1] A copy of this score sheet, with instructions, can be secured by writing to the author at the New York Athletic Club, 180 Central Park So., New York 19, N.Y. Additional copies can be easily run off on a multigraph machine.

it shows the skill of the players in executing these difficult shots and is helpful when writing newspaper releases and also of interest to club and tournament players when placed on a bulletin board so that they can look at and
digest it. The score is clearly shown at all times permitting the referee
to announce the score each time a player starts serving and the total as each
hand is put out.

SEEDING PLAYERS

To those who have had little or no experience in conducting tournaments and championships a few suggestions as to the procedure of the rating
and seeding of players may be of interest. The success of a tournament
depends to a great extent on the proper seeding of the players. As the
tournament progresses the matches should get more interesting and exciting,
since the weaker players are eliminated and the stronger players meet each
other.

The quarterfinals, barring upsets, should have the best eight remaining
players competing for the championship. Spectators watch the draw and,
as the weaker players are eliminated and the stronger ones advance, interest
increases and the gallery fills to see the crowning of the champion.

The tournament committee should be acquainted with the playing
ability, reputation, and ratings of the top-flight players. If not, a player
whose ability is in question should be investigated so as to prevent a
"sleeper" from receiving an unfair advantage.

If the tournament you are about to hold was held the year before, the
seeding should be made in the order in which the players finished. If the
first four or eight players of the previous year's tournament have again
entered, the winner should be seeded No. 1 and placed at the top of the
draw. The runner-up should be seeded No. 2 at the bottom of the draw.
The No. 3 man is at the top of the lower half, and the No. 4 man is placed
at the bottom of the upper half. To extend this seeding of players, if the
fifth, sixth, seventh, and eighth players (quarterfinalists of the previous
year) are also entered, the proper seeding would be as follows (on basis
of thirty-two entries):

> No. 1 player on the top line
> 2 player on the 32nd line
> 3 player on the 17th line
> 4 player on the 16th line
> 5 player on the 24th line
> 6 player on the 8th line
> 7 player on the 25th line
> 8 player on the 9th line

This seeding assures the top eight players from the previous tournament,
barring upsets, of reaching the quarterfinals.

If, for some reason or other, the winner of the previous tournament does not enter this year, then each of the seeded players advances one position. The player advanced to the fourth seeded position should, in the opinion of the committee, be the best player in the previous year's quarterfinals.

A problem may arise if some outstanding player—e.g., one who has a championship rating and did not play in the previous year's tournament—enters this year's tournament. His entry should not in any way change the seeding procedure. The new player should be seeded after the first four of last year's tournament.

THE DRAW

The draw sheet, which shows the names of the players, the club they represent, and who their opponents will be if they win their match, should be drawn up so that all "byes" are shown in the first round. Under no circumstances should any "byes" be extended beyond the first round.

When the number of entries is two, or a power of two (4, 8, 16, 32, 64, 128), then all names can be written down in a single column and two players will meet in the finals. It is only when the total number of entries is not a power of two that complications arise. In such cases, it is necessary to arrange the first round matches so that the winners added to the number of byes will cause the number of players in the second round to equal a power of two. If this is not done, you will have three players left in the finals. Thus, you must prepare to have two players in the finals by placing a certain number of players in the second round. Such players are called "byes," and have one less match to play than the other competitors.

The first step in making the draw is to determine the number of "byes." This is done by subtracting the number of entries from the next higher power of two. For example: Assume that you have 39 entries; subtract 39 from the next higher power of two, which is 64. This leaves 25 byes, 12 placed in the upper half of the draw and 13 in the lower. 14 players are required to play in the first round.

For example:

> 64 minus 39 leaves 25 byes for the second round
> 39 minus 25 leaves 14 players in the first round
> 14 divided by 2 equals 7 winners in the first round
> 7 plus 25 byes equals 32 players in the second round

The winners of the first round are advanced to the second round in line with the 25 byes. You now have 32 players in the second round and only two men can meet in the finals. The object is to bring into the second round a number of players equal to the power of two.

The method of drawing for doubles is identical, except that a pair is substituted for a single player.

A few examples of drawings in which there are byes:

Number of Entries	Number of Players in 1st Round	Number of Byes	Number of Players in 2nd Round
13	10	3	8
24	16	8	16
28	24	4	16
32 no byes			
46	28	18	32
64 no byes			

TOURNAMENT RULES

In championship tournaments—district, state, city—and in many cases for club championships—singles and doubles—where time is a factor, the proper scheduling of the games should be carefully considered. This is particularly true where a player enters both singles and doubles, as many top-flight players do. In such cases a player may be required to play both singles and doubles on the same day or night with very little rest between games. This is a risk a player assumes when he enters both singles and doubles.

In preliminary games, if possible, a player should be given at least a one-hour rest period between the singles and doubles matches.

The Unified Handball Rules recommend, where one or more contestants have reached the finals in both singles and doubles, to play the doubles match on the day preceding the singles. This assures plenty of rest between the final matches. If it is not possible or feasible to do this, and both matches will have to be played on the same day or night, then:

a. The singles match should be played first.
b. A rest period of not more than one hour should be allowed between the finals in singles and doubles.

In championship tournaments the spectators are there and in many cases, have paid admission to see both final matches. To ask them to wait three hours (old rule) between final matches is asking too much. Experience shows that the spectators do not wait, and the match is poorly attended. The one-hour rest period between final matches will keep the fans in their seats and assure a larger audience for the final match. To keep spectator's interest keyed up during this waiting period, a match for third place in the championship, or just an exhibition match, could be put on.

Appendix

In this appendix you will find a synopsis of the Unified Handball Rules adopted in 1958 by the AAU, YMCA, USHA, and the JWB. Space does not permit the showing of the complete rules.

This synopsis is simply a brief condensation of the rules, a general idea of the fundamental rules. A wrong interpretation may be put on a brief outline of some important rule.

It is therefore recommended that beginners particularly, in order to play the game properly and enjoy it, eliminating confusion and misunderstanding, secure a copy of the Unified Handball Rules and read it carefully.

SYNOPSIS OF UNIFIED HANDBALL RULES APPLYING TO BOTH ONE- AND FOUR-WALLS

(Synopsis of Rules for Four-Wall on Page 77)
(Synopsis of Rules for One-Wall on Page 79)

EQUIPMENT

Ball. Black rubber 1⅞ inches in diameter, weight 2.3 ounces, rebound from 70-inch drop 42 to 48 inches at temperature of 68 degrees.

Gloves. Any glove light in color, soft material or leather. Fingers of glove shall not be webbed or connected. No foreign substance, tape, rubber bands used on fingers and palm. Gloves must be worn at all times.

Uniform. White pants, shirt, socks, sneakers.

GAME

A. Only one hand may be used in striking the ball.
B. May be played by two, three (cut throat), or four.
C. Game shall be won by side first scoring 21 points.
D. Match consists of winning two of three games.
E. Points. Only the side serving can score points.
F. Receiver putting server's hand out gains service.
G. After ball is legally served receiver returns the ball by striking it on the first bounce or on the fly so that it will strike the front wall. Server then returns the ball and play continues until either side is unable to return the ball legally, which then constitutes a point or hand out as the case may be.

OFFICIALS

There shall be a Referee who decides all questions. His decisions are in accordance with these rules. His decisions are final. He has the authority to forfeit a match.

When the referee makes his call on any play, play immediately stops and voids any play of the ball that may follow.

SERVICE

a. Toss of a coin decides right to serve first. Winner starts first and third game.
b. When the server or serving side loses the service, he or they become the receiver and the receiver the server and so alternately in all subsequent services of the game.
c. In serving the ball must be bounced on the floor anywhere within the serving zone and struck on its first bounce.
d. If the server attempts to hit the ball on the first rebound and fails, he is out.
e. On serving, the server may not bounce the ball more than three times in the serving zone. Violation retires the server.
f. Server must not serve until opponent is in position.
g. Deliberate delay exceeding ten seconds by server or receiver is a penalty against offender, handout, or point, as the case may be.
h. In doubles the side starting each game is allowed one handout. Thereafter, both men on each team serve.
i. At beginning of each game each team informs the referee which one of them will serve first and this service order is followed throughout that game. Failure to do so counts as a handout and the loss of any points scored during that serve.

RECEIVING SERVICE

Receiver is required to play a legal service either on the fly, or on the first bounce.
Receiver is not permitted to run in over the short line to play a served ball.
The receiver cannot play an illegally served ball.

TIMES OUT

a. During a game each player in singles or each side in doubles either while serving or receiving may request a "time out" for a towel, wiping glasses, etc.
b. Each time out shall not exceed 30 seconds.
c. No more than three time outs in a game are allowed to each singles player or each team in doubles.

REST PERIODS

a. Rest periods of two minutes between the first and second games, at which time players must not leave the court without approval of referee. Not to exceed ten minutes between the second and third games and players may leave the court.
b. In case of injury if player is unable to resume play at end of 15 minutes, match is forfeited.

WET BALL—GLOVES

a. Every effort should be made to keep the ball dry. Deliberate violation of the spirit of this rule shall result in forfeiture of service.
b. Ball may be inspected at any time by referee.
c. If player's glove is wet and referee believes player has an unfair advantage, he shall require the player to change gloves.

In singles, while the ball is in play, if the ball is swung at and completely missed, the player may again attempt to play the ball before the second bounce. In doubles, while the ball is in play, if a player swings at and completely misses the ball, he may again play the ball, or his partner is permitted to play the ball before the second bounce of the ball.

HINDERS

a. A returned ball that strikes an opponent before striking the floor is a "dead ball" and must be played over.
b. In doubles both players on a side are entitled to a fair chance at the ball and either one is entitled to a hinder even though it would naturally be his partner's ball, despite the fact that his partner may be attempting to play the ball or that he may already have missed it.
c. When a player is interfered with by his partner it is not a hinder.

AVOIDABLE HINDERS

a. When a player is blocked intentionally, unnecessarily, or in an unsportsmanlike manner by his opponent it shall be an out or point against the offender.
b. For more detailed information on *hinders* see sections on one-wall and four-wall rules.

FOUR-WALL RULES

(Synopsis of General Rules on Page 75)

COURT SPECIFICATIONS

Standard measurements 20 feet wide, 20 feet high, 40 feet long, backwall 12 feet high.
Short Line. Court divided into a front and a back court of equal dimensions by a line called the *short line* running parallel to the front wall.
Service Line. Five feet in front of short line another parallel line called the *service line.*
Service Zone. Space between outer edges of these two lines is the *service zone.*
Service Box. Eighteen inches from and parallel with each side wall a line shall be drawn to form the *service box.*
Lines. All lines shall be 1½ inches wide, red or yellow.

OFFICIALS

The officials shall be a Referee and a Scorer. For duties of Referee refer to Synopsis of Unified Handball rules, page 75, and Chapter 5.
The Scorer shall keep a correct record of points scored, outs, order of service, announce score frequently.

SERVICE

a. Server drops the ball in serving zone and on the first rebound strikes the ball so that it will first hit the front wall and on the rebound land upon the floor back of the short line either before or after striking one of the side walls.
b. The server must start serving from any place in the service zone.
c. In doubles partner of server must stand in service box with back to the side wall, both feet on the ground while the ball is being served.

FAULTS

Any two of the following in succession puts the server out. When the served ball:
a. hits the front wall and two side walls before striking the floor.
b. hits the front wall and fails to strike back of the short line on the fly.

c. hits front, side, and back walls before striking the floor.

d. rebounds from the front wall and touches the back wall or ceiling before striking the floor.

e. strikes the floor and back wall simultaneously.

Or when

f. server's partner is not in the service box.

g. server steps beyond the service or short line in the act of serving.

h. player's partner standing in service box is hit by a served ball on the bounce—short ball.

DEAD BALL

a. If player's partner, while standing in service box, is hit by a served fly ball, it is ruled a "dead ball" but does not eliminate any short or fault preceding the service.

b. A ball from the front wall on a fly or first bounce that goes into the gallery.

RECEIVER

a. Receiver or receiving side must stand at least five feet back of the short line while the ball is being served.

b. Is not permitted to run in over the short line to play a served ball on the fly.

HINDERS

a. Both players on a side are entitled to a fair and unobstructed chance to play the ball.

b. It is the duty of the side that has played the ball to get out of the way of their opponents. (For more details see page 77, Hinders.)

OUTS

a. Two illegally served balls in succession.

b. An avoidable hinder.

c. A legally served ball touching server on the fly.

d. A legally served ball that strikes server's partner when he is outside the service box.

e. A legally returned ball striking partner of the one returning the ball.

f. Failure of the server or side properly to return a ball in play.

g. Served ball hitting ceiling, floor, or side walls before striking the front wall.

h. If a ball from the front wall on a fly or first bounce goes into the gallery after having been touched by a player.

i. Served ball hitting front and side wall, or front wall and floor, or front wall and ceiling, at the same time (crotch ball).

"SCREEN BALL"

When a served fair ball rebounds from the front wall so close to the server that he obstructs the receiver's view, it is a "screen ball" and ruled as a "dead ball" but does not void any previous short or long ball.

STRADDLED BALL

The referee shall decide whether or not a ball passing between the legs of the player or side having last played the ball shall be ruled as a hinder.

ONE-WALL RULES

(For Synopsis of General Rules See Page 75)

COURT SPECIFICATIONS

Standard measurements: wall 20 feet wide—16 feet high. Floor 20 feet wide 34 feet long from the wall to the back edge of the long line.

Sidelines shall be perpendicular to the wall lines and extended at least three feet further from the wall than the long line.

There should be a minimum of six feet of the floor outside each sideline and in back of long line to allow sufficient movement area for the players.

SHORT LINE

Short line runs parallel with the front wall between the sidelines with its back edge 16 feet from the wall.

SERVICE MARKERS

Service markers (lines) at least six inches long and parallel to and midway between long and short lines extending inward from the sidelines.

SERVICE LINE

The imaginary further extension of these service markers indicates the *service line*.

LINES

All lines shall be 1½ inches in width. Red or yellow is suggested.

SERVICE ZONE

The floor area inside and including the short, side, and service markers.

RECEIVING ZONE

The floor area in back of the short line bounded by and including the side- and long lines.

PLAYING ZONE

The floor area between the front wall and long line and between the sidelines and including these lines.

OFFICIALS

For all champion matches there shall be a referee and four linesmen. One linesman for each sideline, short and long lines.

SERVICE

    a. Server must start serving from any place within the service zone.
    b. Server's partner must stand outside the sidelines astraddle the imaginary service line.
    c. Server's partner must not enter playing zone before the served ball passes him.

Any two of the following serves (a) to (e) in succession put the server out:

a. If while serving any part of the foot extends beyond the serving zone.
b. Partner not astraddle the service line.
c. Partner entering the court too soon.
d. Ball rebounding from the front wall that fails to strike the floor back of the short line and between the sidelines on the fly.
e. Ball rebounding from wall that strikes the floor back of the long line and between the sidelines on the fly.

RECEIVER

Receiver or receivers must stand back of the service line until the ball passes the short line. Cannot play an illegal serve.

OUTS

The server's hand is out:

a. For two illegally served balls in succession.
b. Avoidable hinders.
c. Ball in play striking partner of the one returning the ball.
d. Served ball striking outside the sidelines.
e. Served ball first hitting floor, ceiling, or outside the front wall.
f. Served ball striking the server on the fly.
g. Server attempts to hit the ball on its first rebound and misses.
h. Server bounces the ball more than three times in the service zone in making a service.

HINDERS

a. Unintentional interference with an opponent in such a way as to prevent him from having a fair chance to play the ball.
b. If a player stands perfectly still in front or aside the player it is NOT a hinder. This is considered a legal play.
c. If an opponent backs into the player who may or may not be standing still, it is a hinder. See "hinders" in synopsis of General Rules.

VARIATIONS FOR THREE-WALL COURTS

Throughout the country there are a number of three-wall courts consisting of a front and two side walls (no back walls).

The playing rules for these courts are the same as those for four-wall with the exception that a ball in play, striking outside the long line, is a point or handout, as the case may be. A service ball striking outside the long line is a long ball. Two long balls, or one long and one short in succession, put the server out.

Spectators are limited to the area behind the long line, thus allowing for sufficient space to permit players to return the ball in play while standing in back of the long line.

The new *jai-alai* type three-wall courts have the same playing area as the standard four-wall courts—20 feet wide, 40 feet long, and 20 feet high. A 1½-inch line is drawn on the open side of the court from the front to the back wall, called the "outside" line. The court is divided in equal dimensions, lengthwise, by a line called the short line, running parallel with the front wall. A "service" line and "service" box are drawn similar to those on four-wall courts. With the "short" line dividing the court in equal dimensions, the front wall of the first game is used as the back wall for the second game with the players simply switching around in serving each game. This plan eliminates any advantage a player who has a strong right or left hand may have over a player with a weak left or right hand.

The playing rules are easily followed. The present Unified Handball Rules for Four-Wall cover shorts, service, longs, and receiving, while the one-wall rules apply to all balls striking on or outside lines.

Glass side walls, back wall, and gallery of the "all-glass" court in the YMCA at Aurora, Ill. Both side walls and back wall are of glass panels so that with the gallery space over 600 spectators can get an excellent view of the game. This is the only all-glass handball court in the United States and, in fact, in the world.

Courts at the YMCA at Benton Harbor, Mich., showing back walls with glass panels permitting an excellent view of the entire court.

In addition to excellent playing facilities the court at the Denver Downtown YMCA with the upper part of each side wall of glass affords the spectators an excellent close-up view of the play.

Overflow crowd of some four to five hundred spectators watches a game between Carl Obert and Marty Decatur on the three-wall jai-alai handball court in Lincoln Terrace Park in Brooklyn, N.Y. The open side brings spectators close to the play where they can easily follow the ball and enjoy watching the skills and techniques of the players.

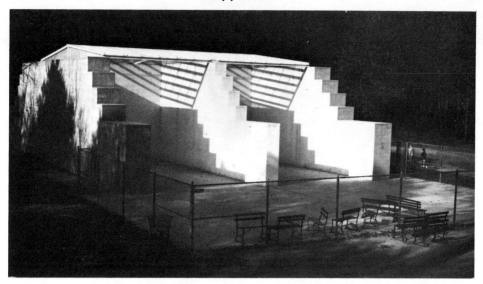

Three-wall outdoor courts, front and two side walls, in Palmer Park, Detroit, Mich. Each year over the Labor Day holiday a national tournament is held that attracts many of the nation's outstanding four-wall players.

One of the large, 24 by 48 feet courts at the New York Athletic Club remodeled to the standard 20 by 40 feet size. Left side wall solid construction 12 feet high—glass panels six feet high—two feet above glass panels solid construction. This additional gallery space accommodates about forty to fifty spectators, permitting a close-up view of all the plays. With the large gallery space in the back of the court, as many as two hundred people can be taken care of.

One-wall handball court, Brownsville Boy's Club, Brooklyn, N.Y. With about 95% of all one-wall handball courts in and around the Metropolitan area in New York City outdoors, there are many excellent indoor courts available. This court is about the best in the city and can accommodate close to one thousand spectators who have a close-up view of the game and can follow the skills, shots, and court coverings of the players. The picture shows an excellent play by Ken Davidoff in a game with Oscar Obert in the foreground. The lines on the floor are a little confusing, as some of them are the lines of the basketball court. The handball court lines are those straight lines extending from the front wall to the heavy line extending across the court about three feet or so in back of Ken Davidoff. (Picture taken by Martin Schneider and shown here through the courtesy of the USHA.)

"IN AND OUT" SCORING

The author has no intention of suggesting any change in the scoring rule, particularly for national, state, or district championships, although some day a change may be desirable. However, for club championships and "pick-up" games at your club or "Y" this "In and Out" scoring method may be of interest.

Under the present scoring rule "ONLY THE SERVING SIDE CAN SCORE POINTS." It is quite common in tournaments where players are about equal in playing ability for a match of three games to continue from 1½ to 2 hours and longer. These long games are very exhausting on the players—the match is slowed up by the players' using every device to rest—playing time schedules may be disrupted causing confusion and delays.

For the purpose of speeding the play, reducing materially the present average time consumed for matches for both singles and doubles, to reduce the danger of time schedule snags and delays, to conserve the stamina of players, to assure faster and more interesting games without handicapping in any way a player's skills and ability, and to keep spectators more interested, I would suggest for club class A, B, and C tournaments and for "pick-up" games experimentation with this "In and Out" scoring plan.

Under "In and Out" scoring plan points can be scored by the server during serve and by the receiver when he puts the server's hand out. Study this plan a little and I believe that you will agree that it has some merit and is fair to all players. It would be particularly helpful in tournaments with large entry lists that have to be completed in a short time.

Let me illustrate this scoring plan for a game of singles. Player A starts serving and makes two points. Player B, the receiver, then puts A's hand out, B is credited with a point for putting A's hand out and the right to serve. The score when B starts to serve is A, 1 and B, 2. B on his serve makes four points. A then puts B out and receives a point. The score when A again starts to serve: A, 3; B, 5, and so on until the first player makes 21 points. Every time that the server's hand is put out the receiver gets a point and the right to serve. If the server should put his own hand out under the rules (two shorts, longs, etc.), the receiver would receive a point and the right to serve.

Assume that both players have 20 points. Extra pressure is put on the server to make the point, for if he fails and the receiver puts him out (or the server puts his own hand out), the receiver scores a point and wins the game. In doubles the receivers gain two points each time that they put both of the servers' hands out. Under the present scoring rule there are many interesting matches where the score is say 21 to 10, which would indicate an easy game. The score does not reflect the hard-fought defensive game and the excellent play of the loser. The loser may have put the winner's hand out six or seven times by well-executed shots but has received no credit for these shots except the right to serve. It seems to me that he should receive greater reward for his fine playing by receiving a point every time he puts the server's hand out. In other words, under this "In and Out" scoring rule each player receives credit for all of his well-played shots while serving and receiving.

This "In and Out" scoring plan where players are about equal in ability would not favor any one player over another or give any advantage to any player. It has been said that an "underdog" player in a match has a slight advantage when he receives a point each time he puts the server's hand out. I don't believe that there is much substance to this as the better player has the same advantage when he completes a hand out. The "underdog's" slight advantage is more than offset by the many advantages in time-saving and interest that this scoring rule has over the present one. It speeds up games and makes courts available faster, particularly on days when all courts are in use and players are waiting to play.

Glossary

ACE—A legally served ball that completely eludes the receiver.

CROTCH BALL—A ball hitting at the juncture of any two flat surfaces, such as the front wall and ceiling, floor and side wall, or in the corners.

DEAD BALL—Any ball out of play without penalty.

FAULT—An illegally served ball that involves a penalty.

FIST BALL—A ball struck with a closed fist.

HANDOUT—The loss of serve, when the server fails to serve legally, or the serving side fails to return a ball legally in play.

HINDER—An accidental interference or obstruction of the flight of the ball not involving a penalty.

HOOK—A ball breaking to the left or right after it strikes the floor.

HOP—See Hook.

KILL—A ball returned to the wall in such a manner that it rebounds from the front wall so close to the floor that it is impossible to return legally.

LONG—A served ball that, in one-wall, strikes the floor in back of the long line; in four-wall that first strikes the front wall and back wall before striking the floor.

LONG LINE—In one-wall, a line running parallel to and 34 feet from the front wall marking the end of the court.

POINT—A tally scored by the serving side.

PUNCH—See Fist Ball.

RALLY—The play after service until one side fails legally to return the ball.

RECEIVER—The player or players to whom the ball is served.

SCREEN BALL—A served ball that passes so close to the server that he obstructs the receiver's view of the ball.

SERVER—The player serving the ball.

SERVICE BOX—The area in three- and four-wall doubles where the partner stands while the ball is being served.

SERVICE ZONE—The court area from which the server is required to serve the ball.

SERVING SIDE—In doubles, the server and his partner.

SETUP—A ball in play that gives the player an easy opportunity for a kill or passing shot, etc.

SHORT—An illegally served ball that after striking the front wall does not pass the short line on the fly.

SHORT LINE—A line running parallel to the front wall. In four-wall, it is midway between the front and back walls. In one-wall it is 16 feet from the front wall.

SIDE OUT—Loss of service by the serving side.

VOLLEY—See Rally.